Also from Westphalia Press
westphaliapress.org

The Idea of the Digital University

Dialogue in the Roman-Greco World

The Politics of Impeachment

International or Local Ownership?: Security Sector Development in Post-Independent Kosovo

Policy Perspectives from Promising New Scholars in Complexity

The Role of Theory in Policy Analysis

ABC of Criminology

Non-Profit Organizations and Disaster

The Idea of Neoliberalism: The Emperor Has Threadbare Contemporary Clothes

Donald J. Trump's Presidency: International Perspectives

Ukraine vs. Russia: Revolution, Democracy and War: Selected Articles and Blogs, 2010-2016

Iran: Who Is Really In Charge?

Stamped: An Anti-Travel Novel

A Strategy for Implementing the Reconciliation Process

Issues in Maritime Cyber Security

A Different Dimension: Reflections on the History of Transpersonal Thought

Contracting, Logistics, Reverse Logistics: The Project, Program and Portfolio Approach

Unworkable Conservatism: Small Government, Freemarkets, and Impracticality

Springfield: The Novel

Lariats and Lassos

Ongoing Issues in Georgian Policy and Public Administration

Growing Inequality: Bridging Complex Systems, Population Health and Health Disparities

Designing, Adapting, Strategizing in Online Education

Secrets & Lies in the United Kingdom: Analysis of Political Corruption

Pacific Hurtgen: The American Army in Northern Luzon, 1945

Natural Gas as an Instrument of Russian State Power

New Frontiers in Criminology

Feeding the Global South

Beijing Express: How to Understand New China

Demand the Impossible: Essays in History as Activism

Uganda in Transformation, 1876-1926

by
Herbert Gresford Jones, D.D.

WESTPHALIA PRESS
An imprint of Policy Studies Organization

Uganda in Transformation, 1876-1926

All Rights Reserved © 2023 by Policy Studies Organization

Westphalia Press
An imprint of Policy Studies Organization
1527 New Hampshire Ave., NW
Washington, D.C. 20036
info@ipsonet.org

ISBN-13: 978-1-63723-626-0

Cover design by Jeffrey Barnes:
jbarnesbook.design

Daniel Gutierrez-Sandoval, Executive Director
PSO and Westphalia Press

Updated material and comments on this edition
can be found at the Westphalia Press website:
www.westphaliapress.org

UGANDA IN TRANSFORMATION

IN THE SHADOW OF ST. PAUL'S CATHEDRAL, NAMIREMBE
BOYS OF BUDO SCHOOL AT PHYSICAL DRILL

[*Frontispiece*

UGANDA IN TRANSFORMATION
1876-1926

BY THE RIGHT REVEREND
HERBERT GRESFORD JONES, D.D.

CHURCH MISSIONARY SOCIETY,
6 SALISBURY SQUARE, LONDON, E.C.4
1926

*Made and Printed in Great Britain by
The Camelot Press Limited
London and Southampton*

PREFACE

IN no sense is this little book a historical record. It only attempts in a series of pen pictures to convey the impressions of one who for a while had unusual opportunities of insight into certain portions of the work. In the selection of these pictures I have been guided primarily by the course of personal observation. On this account the more recently developed eastern portion of the Protectorate predominates unduly over the western, the side that witnessed the conflict and pain of the early days. There are great and obvious omissions. Some of the main features and outstanding personalities in the country are barely indicated. Yet in the same way that the inspiration of a journey may to a certain extent remain in the snapshot photographs that we bring home, so perhaps these slight sketches may convey something of the appeal of this child race as it struggles to find its feet in its great and lonely country.

Already there is a small library of books upon the development of Uganda. To a number of those that I have consulted acknowledgment is attempted in the text. Dr. Eugene Stock's " History of the C.M.S." must remain for the Uganda Mission an unrivalled record. With the small group of works that may be termed classical, must also be ranked Sir Frederick Lugard's " Dual Mandate in British Tropical Africa " and Sir Harry Johnston's " Colonization of Africa."

The one section of this present volume that we have tried, with the invaluable help of Canon G. K. Baskerville, to make complete is the Roll, in itself an inspiration, of those who have served in the Uganda Mission since 1877. To those who have gone before and to those who come after, but most of all to the little company whom I have been privileged to call my fellow workers I would inscribe this small volume.

H. G. J.

PERSHORE,
October, 1926.

CONTENTS

CHAP.		PAGE
I.	INTO THE HEART OF AFRICA	1
II.	SOME OUTSTANDING MEMORIES	15
III.	TRANSFORMATION	46
IV.	EXPANSION WESTWARD	69
V.	BUSOGA	87
VI.	MOUNT ELGON AND THE MASS MOVEMENT	97
VII.	TESO AND THE NEW MODEL	115
VIII.	LANGO : A STUDY IN ANIMISM	130
IX.	UGANDA'S GIFT TO THE SUDAN	140
X.	ADVANCING ON OTHER FRONTS	158
XI.	UNDER THE RED CROSS	166
XII.	AFRICAN EDUCATION	175
XIII.	SOME PROBLEMS OF MIDDLE AFRICA	193
XIV.	CO-TRUSTEES	228
XV.	FUTURE LEADERSHIP	234

APPENDICES

I.	SOME NOTABLE DATES IN THE HISTORY OF UGANDA	254
II.	BISHOPS AND ADMINISTRATORS	256
III.	ROLL OF MISSIONARIES	257
IV.	RECENT BOOKS ON UGANDA	261

MAPS AND ILLUSTRATIONS

IN THE SHADOW OF ST. PAUL'S
CATHEDRAL, NAMIREMBE . *Frontispiece*
PAGE
MAP OF THE TWO ROADS TO UGANDA 14
SKETCH PLAN OF NAMIREMBE HILL . 57
MAP OF THE UGANDA PROTECTORATE 70
MAP OF BUSOGA AND THE EASTERN
PROVINCE 86
MAP OF UGANDA AND THE SUDAN . 114
MAP OF THE NILE VALLEY, SHOWING
THE FOUR DIOCESES . . . 129

UGANDA IN TRANSFORMATION

CHAPTER I

INTO THE HEART OF AFRICA

I

UNTIL fifty years ago the centre of Africa was left severely alone. Like some haunted chamber in a great mansion it stood among the habitations of men—remote, mysterious, unprobed. If haply some adventurous traveller made bold to intrude into its recesses, he was fêted on his return to civilization as one who had dared great deeds. The very globes and maps of our grandparents reflected this general aloofness. Rivers, clearly marked near the coast, emerged from dotted lines inland. Vague surmises hazarded the outlines of lakes or mountains. Blank spaces for the most part indicated the "Great Unknown."

A short half-century and all is changed. By a transformation—one of the most remarkable in human history—Middle Africa has become another "New World." The dark continent has been found to be a land of sunshine. The mystery regions of famous explorers offer to-day metalled roads to the common motorist. Messrs. Sifton and Praed can as easily furnish him with a road map of Uganda as they can of North Wales. The uncharted expanses of a generation past now give cause for pre-occupation to cabinet ministers, or hold open doors of expectation to the leaders of commerce. The human occupants of these veiled territories, far from proving enemies to civilized man, are found to be his ready co-operators. They who a while ago were deemed to be but objects of missionary compassion are now accorded an imperial educational policy. The stone that so recently the builders rejected has become, if not the headstone of the corner, at least a very serviceable portion of the whole structure.

What we venture therefore to term the Uganda Jubilee may well claim a general measure of public attention. To a wide circle of readers, whether their interests are ethnological, commercial, administrative or religious, it will be no small matter of interest to inquire what are the causes and what the processes by which this remarkable change in Middle Africa has been brought about.

The Uganda of to-day is the outcome of the combined efforts of colonists, travellers, and above all of Christian missionaries. The name of the continent is itself significant. The suggestion of Servius, the scholiast on Virgil, that it is derived from *aprica*, sunny, much as some of us would welcome it, is untenable. The language of Carthage, that ancient colony of Tyre, supplies a more natural explanation, for the word *Afrygah* means a colony. The Phœnicians may have spoken of their Afrygah as we do of our colonies.

First and foremost, as was most natural, there came in by the ever-open door of the Nile Delta those whose race gave rise to the dynasties, the commerce, the art, and the glory of ancient Egypt. The Phœnicians next, and after them the Romans, discovered the possibilities of Africa, only to found colonies along the northern coast and in the rich valley of the Nile.

The people from whom we derive the first information concerning the interior of Africa are the Arabs, who by means of the camel were able to penetrate across the great desert to the very centre of the continent, and by ships to trade along the two coasts as far as the Senegal and the Gambia on the west and Mombasa on the east. The fifteenth century marked a new era in maritime discovery. The voyages of the Portuguese inspired by Henry the Navigator were the first to give anything like an accurate outline of the two coasts, and to complete the circumnavigation of Africa. The discovery of America and the West India Islands gave rise to the infamous traffic in African negroes, and thus incidentally further knowledge of the west coast was secured. With the English and French settlements in Africa began a systematic survey of the coast and portions of the interior.

As a " colony " Africa became known to civilization. A vast field for colonization she has remained. When the " scramble for Africa " was terminated by the Treaty of Berlin (1885) the only independent powers that survived the partition were the kingdom of Abyssinia on the east and the little republic of Liberia on the west.

II

It is not, however, the resources of the continent itself, it is its peoples that count most in its development. A tropical world of swamp, forest, and scrub, a world of glare and heat, of malaria and plague, while it may sternly repel the intruder, may readily yield the riches of its produce to those indigenous to its soil.

Who are these people, and whence have they come ? The answer is one upon which ethnologists are slow to agree. The original home of the negroid peoples is unknown. Man probably entered Africa from Syria, drawn on, so it would seem, by the search for the larger mammals. Along the equator and to the south of it are to be found the Bantu negroes, bound together in one linguistic group that includes Banyoro, Baganda, Zulus, and Hottentots. To the north of these are the tall, long-limbed Nilotic tribes to be found east of the Nile, from the Bantu line in Kenya and Uganda, up to the southernmost habitations of Arabs in El Obeid and Kordofan.

The Congo pygmy and the forest negro of Middle Africa appear to be the most primitive of the negroid type. Farther again to the north and to the east are the Hamitic races. Under this term the modern ethnologist groups the earlier occupants of the valley of the Nile, Egyptian, Copt, and Abyssinian, an influx conceivably from the Caucasus or Mesopotamia and possibly white in colour. Traces of their influence at the heart of Africa to-day are the long-horned ox, the hump-backed ox, the fat-tailed sheep, the Nubian ass, and the domestic fowl. The art of boat-building, the carving of stools and head-rest pillows, and the prevalence of some few games of chance come also from them. In the main, however, the mighty builders and conquerors of dynastic Egypt seem to have penetrated little farther to the south than the northern Sudan. The humbler dwellers at the head of their great valley seem to have been left untouched.

If it was to the zeal of the early colonists that we owe the knowledge of the coast of Africa, it is to the intrepidity and persistence of the great travellers that we are indebted for our first serious contact with the many tribes and races of her vast interior.

So great, in fact, was the uncertainty that prevailed in the geography of the interior of Africa up to the end of the eighteenth century, that in 1788 there was formed in London an association of learned and scientific men with a view to its exploration. As an outcome of this movement fresh discoveries were made in rapid succession. For the next fifty years investigation centred largely in the west and in the north of the continent. From 1795 to 1805 Mungo Park added much to what was known of the Niger basin. Hornemann, Denham, Bruce, Browne, and others, from 1796 to 1840, threw fresh light upon the Sahara and the valley of the Nile.

On the eastern side as regards the interior all was yet in obscurity. At Mombasa, the colonist had been already active. Here to this day the Fort of Jesus, standing up above the old harbour, speaks of early Portuguese possession in the sixteenth century. Here in 1844 a mission was founded by the Church Missionary Society, and it is to two of its first missionaries there, Dr. Krapf and Mr. Rebmann, that the first discoveries in East Africa are due. In 1848 Rebmann discovered the snow-clad dome of Kilima-njaro Krapf, taking a more northerly route, came upon Kenya, the peak that stands up majestically within sight of Nairobi, and that now gives its name to what until 1920 was called British East Africa. They also reported the existence of vast inland lakes beyond these mountains, which awakened great interest at home. It was in consequence of their reports that, in 1857, under the auspices of the Royal Geographical Society, in which the earlier association had been merged, Captain Speke started inland from Zanzibar. To his memorable journeys, first with Captain Burton, and then later in 1860 with Colonel Grant, we owe our early acquaintance with Uganda.

On 3 August, 1858, Speke came upon what he described as the vast expanse of the pale waters of a great lake, or *nyanza*. Looking northward no land was to be seen, and his native guide, throwing forward his right hand and making repeated snaps of his fingers, endeavoured to indicate something immeasurable beyond. Speke presently was informed by some Arab traders that on the farther shore there was a country called Uganda. He named the vast lake the Victoria Nyanza. " What a field," he wrote, " is open to the world, if England does not neglect this discovery." Four years later, in 1862, Speke travelled round the western side of the lake, entered Uganda, and stayed there for some months with King Mtesa. He then discovered the source of the Nile at Jinja, tracing its stream to Gondokoro; and so, with Sir Samuel Baker, linked up the geography of East Africa with that known through earlier explorers from the Egyptian side.

While we have thus made contact geographically with Uganda through the journey of Captain Speke, it is to the great name of David Livingstone that we must now turn in order to trace what we may call the discovery of its people. With the labours and discoveries of David Livingstone (born 1813, died 1873) we are not immediately concerned. No single explorer has done so much for African geography as Livingstone. His journeys, ranging from the Cape nearly to the equator, covered one-third of the continent. But they did not bring him to Uganda itself. What we owe to Livingstone supremely is the awakening of England to the pathos, the needs, and the possibilities of the African peoples. Incidentally what Uganda owes to him is the advent of H. M. Stanley. Stanley, sent out by Mr. Gordon Bennett of the "New York Herald," had saved the life of Livingstone at Ujiji on 18 October, 1871. It was his letter in the "Daily Telegraph" of 15 November, 1875, that was as a spark to kindle the emotions of Englishmen, already stirred by Livingstone's endeavours, and to give to the Church of Christ the incentive to send forth that mission to Uganda which is the subject of these pages.

III

The story of the Christian Church in Africa must cause to the defender of Christianity many searchings of heart. To any in the apostolic age venturing upon predictions of Christian expansion, Africa might well seem to challenge an immediate evangelization. It was into the moulds ready prepared by the piety and the discipline of Judaism around the Mediterranean that the molten metal of the new religion was evidently designed to run. In this *preparatio evangelii* the northern shores of Africa had no insignificant share. From the Roman provinces of Cyrene and of Egypt a number of " devout men," adherents of Judaism, were present on the great day of Pentecost. Inspired by that signal outpouring of the Spirit, they would return enthusiastic to their own people. Had not one of their number had the high honour, as they would now see it, of bearing the Redeemer's cross ? Had not the Saviour Himself been domiciled awhile in His infancy in the delta of the Nile ? Was not Egypt, then as now, one of the great strategic points of civilization ? Did not Alexandria, with its commerce and its learning, its prestige and its position, constitute a providential base, if not for a world-wide, at least for an African diffusion of the new Gospel? And was not the African Church of that first age rich beyond any other in the teachers that were required for a big movement? The bishopric of Alexandria, as founded by St. Mark, was known as the "Evangelical see." In the Nile Delta, in an unparalleled succession of doctors and bishops, were Origen and Clement, Cyril and Athanasius. "The head of the Alexandrian Church," says Gregory Nazianzus, "is the head of the world." At Carthage, sister metropolis to Alexandria, was Augustine himself. Frumentius was consecrated by Athanasius as missionary bishop for Abyssinia. Martyrs there were, such as St. Catherine; hermits and saints of exceptional piety, like Antony. On the face of things the African Church might indeed have led the world. Was it that in that day, even as till so recently in our own, the Church had no missionary conscience? Was it that theological niceties and party spirit absorbed her attention? What happened? Sir Harry Johnston, in his book "The Colonization of Africa," utters a memorable warning. None, he declares, is quicker than the African either to accept or to lose Christianity. The tide of Moslem invasion of the seventh century, that found in Europe the stuff that could stem it, carried almost everything before it in Africa. What remained, to judge by the Coptic and Abyssinian Christianity of a later day, may have been atrophied and stereotyped.

In the late Middle Ages a fresh expression of zeal was displayed by the Portuguese. Everywhere that their voyages took them the Cross was planted. But in their evangelistic efforts, such as they were, and even in the later missions that may be called the first of modern times, the field of enterprise was narrowed to the coastline. The eighteenth century witnessed, it is true, some inland efforts on the part of Huguenot and Moravian missions, and in the time of Mohammed Ali an Austrian mission penetrated to the Sudan, but in the main the coastal limitation prevailed. In 1787 Sierra Leone felt the influence of John Wesley. In 1799 the Church Missionary Society was founded, and work was begun in Sierra Leone. In 1821 the Society for the Propagation of the Gospel sent clergy to Cape Town.

It was reserved, as we have just seen, for David Livingstone to awaken British sympathies to the "open sore" of Central Africa, and noble was the response of the Universities of Oxford and Cambridge at Zanzibar, and of the Scottish Presbyterians at Blantyre. It was thus upon the ears of a Church awakened to fresh spiritual life through the religious stirring of the nineteenth century, already sensitive to the sufferings of the inland African tribes, that the appeal of H. M. Stanley came with such force. Here at last, upon the evidence of a recognized authority, at the heart of this long-neglected continent, there was a tribe of singular development and promise, through no less a personality than its king asking for instructors. Now at length might the forces of Christ, that for such centuries had tarried, that so long had lingered upon the threshold of Africa, carry forward the Cross and plant it at its very core.

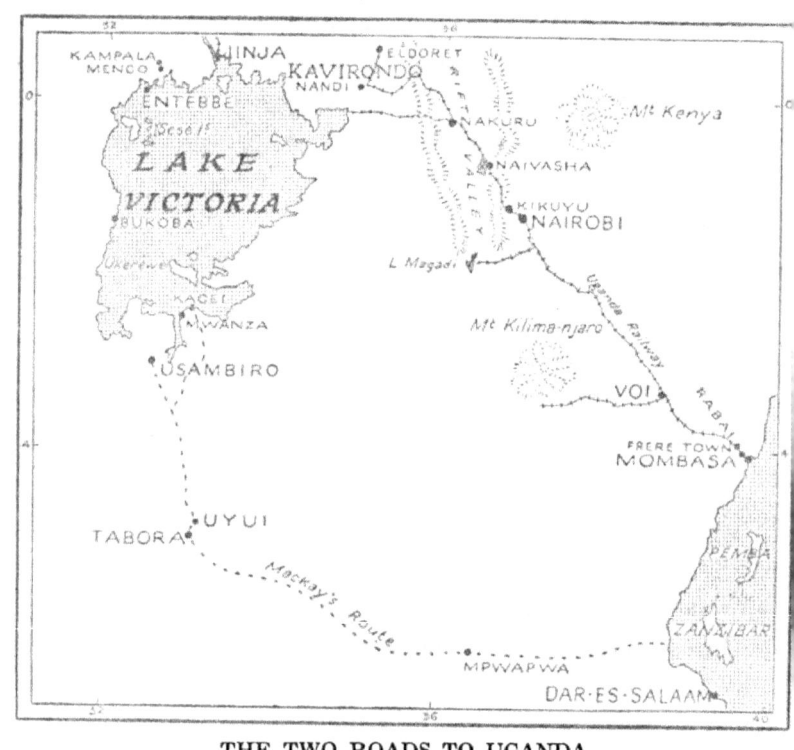

THE TWO ROADS TO UGANDA

The dotted line shows the earlier road used 1877-90; Bishop Tucker's route, 1890, was approximately that indicated by the Uganda Railway.

The Tanganyika Railway now, of course, connects Tabora with Dar-es-Salaam.

CHAPTER II

Some Outstanding Memories

UGANDA during the last fifty years has been no backwater in the world's affairs. If in its earlier stages the renaissance of Central Africa is due to the quiet persistence of geographical societies and intrepid explorers, its later phases have been inextricably intertwined with some of the most stirring happenings both in Church and State. From the religious standpoint Uganda, as we now know it, is one of the chief products of that later evangelical zeal that was so remarkably rekindled in the 'seventies and 'eighties of the Victorian era. It is not, indeed, too much to claim that the romance of the Uganda Mission has to a large extent, both in England and America, inspired that world-wide missionary movement that has been so marked a feature of the last half-century. Politically Uganda during this period has felt the repercussion of some of the more notable events in modern history. The Berlin Agreement of 1885, the incorporation of the British

East Africa Company in 1888, the further Berlin Convention of 1890, the rise of the Mahdi, the fall of Khartoum, the later conquest of the Sudan, and, more recently still, the great war, with its consequent Treaty of Versailles, have successively affected her development. The story has been so often and so ably told that, absorbing as it must always be from both a spiritual and an administrative point of view, it is not the purpose of this volume to traverse it afresh. All that we need attempt is to recall certain memories which make the present occasion to be one of signal interest, and which lead the mind almost inevitably to a profound acknowledgment of the hand of God.

The past fifty years in Uganda fall into two slightly unequal periods. The year 1899, that was to witness the beginning of so much unrest in South Africa, saw throughout all East Africa the coming of a new reign of peace and progress. It marked in the Sudan the termination of the Mahdi's misrule, and the proclamation by Lord Kitchener of the "Agreement" under which that vast territory has prospered ever since. Similarly in Uganda, 1899 saw the last of the machinations of King Mwanga and the confirmation

by Sir Harry Johnston of another memorable
"Agreement," which, whatever its defects, has been recognized by the Uganda chiefs as their Magna Charta from that day to this. With the new century, moreover, Uganda was to find direct access by means of the railway to the outer world. It was to launch out upon its great agricultural future. Best of all, it was to experience that unprecedented spiritual expansion in all directions, east and west and north and south, which it is my present aim to record.

Of the earlier phase of suffering and heroism we must briefly remind ourselves. The years 1877 to 1884 give us the first impact of Christianity upon Central Africa. The period 1884 to 1890 marks the dark night of persecution. With the 'nineties comes the dawn of religious and political organization. For the first period the controlling native influence was that of Mtesa; for the second and third that of Mwanga. One pictures Mtesa as senile and bewildered, though at times amiable : Mwanga as young and vicious and fundamentally hostile. From 1877 to 1899 we find an almost unalleviated sequence of religious and political intrigues, never terminated until the expatriation of Mwanga in 1899. The Rev. R. P. Ashe, in describing this disturbed introductory period in "Two Kings of Uganda," plainly indicates what was with regard to native life the determining factor. To appreciate, however, the full strain and anxiety of those early days, we have to retain in our minds that combination of other influences—Roman Catholic, Mohammedan, and political— which, although separate currents, flowed like a strong tide counter to the progress of the Anglican mission.

It is before this ever-shifting background of fear, suspicion, and intrigue that the main characters of those first days stand out now before our eyes with such conspicuous brightness. In the Royal Navy in Nelson's day it was claimed that every man was a hero. The same might truly be said of the early Church in Uganda. The more you read the well-known story the more you desire to delineate afresh each actor on that wonderful evangelistic stage. In this brief record we can but recover to ourselves some of the great moments, certain of the central leaders. More particularly we shall note the arrival of Shergold Smith and C. T. Wilson at the court of Mtesa ; the heroic endurance of Alexander Mackay, sometimes with Pearson, O'Flaherty, or Ashe, sometimes quite alone,

Some Outstanding Memories 19

through Mwanga's persecution; the death of Bishop Hannington; and the advent of Bishop Tucker with his strong reinforcements.

I

Picture, then, first the familiar scene that more particularly dates this jubilee, the coming of the two Englishmen to Mengo on 30 June, 1877. Two years before, H. M. Stanley had arrived in Uganda, and found Mtesa, its king, exactly as Speke had described him thirteen years earlier. At the end of Stanley's historic letter to the " Daily Telegraph," that reached England ultimately by the Nile route, he added these significant words : " O that some pious practical missionary would come here ! . . . Such an one, if he can be found, would become the saviour of Africa. Nowhere is there in all the pagan world a more promising field for a mission than Uganda. Here, gentlemen, is your opportunity. Embrace it ! The people on the shores of the Nyanza call upon you." Such a challenge was not likely to pass unheeded by the Christian Church. Within a few days no less than £24,000 was subscribed, Mr. Wilson of Sheffield, who then anonymously styled himself "an unprofitable servant," giving the first £5000. The event we now commemorate was the direct result.

We look back to-day across half a century to this arrival of the two white men at the old king's stockade in the middle of Africa. Eight had started from Zanzibar: Lieut. George Shergold Smith, late of the Royal Navy; Alexander Mackay, a Scots engineer; the Rev. C. T. Wilson, a Manchester curate; T. O'Neill, an architect; John Smith, a doctor in the Edinburgh Medical Mission; G. J. Clark, another engineer; W. M. Robertson, an artisan; and James Robertson, a builder. Except for the one clergyman this was veritably " a laymen's mission." It was a venture of no ordinary kind. The long southern route, through what is now Tanganyika Territory, laid a ruinous toll upon the little company. James Robertson died. Mackay, Clark, and W. M. Robertson were invalided back. Only four reached the great Lake at Kagei, and here, on 11 May, 1877, John Smith, the only doctor of the party, also died. O'Neill, the architect, was left behind at the south of the lake with the heavy stuff. The naval officer and the clergyman arrived alone at their destination.

We can easily picture, especially if we have

Some Outstanding Memories

been in Mengo, this opening scene. The *kabaka's lubiri* (king's court), whatever its other limitations, is suitably staged. The straight and spacious avenue by which it is approached lends all the dignity of a Mall or a Corso to the royal domain; and up this roadway, to the accompaniment of curious throngs, and the beatings of drums, and runnings to and fro, we can imagine Shergold Smith and C. T. Wilson ushered into Mtesa's presence. The Baganda excel in such receptions, and Mtesa was then all friendliness. So far so good.

What is more difficult for the ordinary person to realize is the power of endurance necessary to face those long days and weeks and months and years that ensued. Life must first be maintained. Lodging and food must be found under conditions of baffling difficulty. Contact must be made with men of another race. Suspicion and fear must be allayed. Yet all this is but the beginning of the achievement. Even to-day, amid all that has made the life of a European in Central Africa an accepted possibility, there is that about aloneness in the jungle which is eerie and oppressive. Uncivilized man can do so little to supply the mental and moral needs of his civilized brother. The unknown speech rises up like a high wall of partition at every turn. The haunting nature of the atmosphere, especially in the hours of dusk and darkness, seems to shroud the whole personality with some brooding sense of near and desolating evil. All this, day after day.

Worse was soon to come. Shergold Smith must needs rejoin O'Neill to bring up the stores, and both were killed by a suspicious chief. C. T. Wilson was thus left utterly alone. One day it will be the unestimated heroisms that will be found to have counted most in the world's story. It will be the solitary defenders of the beleaguered position whose chivalry will shine out with most lustre. Upon such an one the story of Uganda at its outset rests. It is when we see this young Manchester curate entirely alone, building and battling, with all the obstacles of language, strangeness, and weakness hemming him in, yet triumphing over them, translating, teaching, loving these African chiefs and their people—that we are filled with reverence and wonder. Alone yet not alone, enduring as seeing Him Who is invisible, C. T. Wilson became the rock upon which the Church of Christ in Uganda was first to be built.

II

Wilson's long and lonely vigil was at length relieved by the arrival in November, 1878, of Alexander Mackay, the man destined to shepherd the flock of God in Uganda through the hour of its most fiery trial, and never once to leave the heart of Africa before he died at the south of the Great Lake some twelve years later.

In Alexander Mackay "that Christian Bayard," as Lord Rosebery called him, the Church in Uganda will permanently do honour to one of her most illustrious heroes. He was born in an Aberdeenshire manse in 1849. The year before Rebmann of the C.M.S. had discovered Kilima-njaro; and now Livingstone, in sighting Lake Ngami, had inaugurated his long series of remarkable discoveries. Dr. Mackay, the Highland minister, was noting the new find on his map when Annie, the nurse, entered with the proud news of his son's birth. "The gospel banner," said the minister, " will yet be planted at the very heart of this continent, although not likely in your day or mine, Annie." " But may be in yer son's, sir," quietly replied the old servant, " and wha will say he'll nae hae a han' in it ?"

Mackay was born to a missionary's life. With his mother's earliest teaching he imbibed sympathy with the aspirations of the backward races of the world. At the age of 8 he was a printer, quoting to his father the saying of Luther that "printing is the latest and greatest gift by which God enables us to advance the things of the Gospel." As a boy he was a devourer of books, though every spare hour was spent in the smithy or carpenter's shop, handling tools of all kinds. At 15 we see him at the Aberdeen Grammar School. At 18 he is at the Free Church training college for teachers in Edinburgh, studying engineering at the University at the same time. Next, with a letter in his pocket to Dr. Bonar, Court Chaplain in Berlin, we see him landing on 1 November, 1873, at Hamburg, to learn German and to qualify himself fully as an engineer. It was there in Germany that Henry Wright's appeal in 1875 for pioneer missionaries for Uganda caught his eye. The same night that he first read the appeal he offered his services, and on 27 April, 1876, he sailed for Zanzibar.

Of Mackay's life and work in Uganda volumes have been written, and have been read by thousands. It is no purpose of this present work to trace his adventurous course. Enough that after disheartening hindrances of different kinds he at length arrived in Uganda at the age of 29, and for the next twelve years, amid incredible difficulties and dangers, toiled unceasingly to instruct and protect its people and to kindle in them a personal affection for his Lord and Master.

Of these twelve years six were under Mtesa, six under Mwanga. In Mtesa he had to deal with an old man, nurtured in paganism and slow to part with its customs, who, while welcoming what the European could contribute in material things, was frankly perplexed by the rival claims of Protestant, Roman, and Arab theology. In Mwanga he was face to face with a young profligate whose hand was stretched out to exterminate both Christian teaching and the Christians themselves.

What is more particularly pertinent to this survey is to appraise those gifts of permanent worth which Mackay bestowed upon the Uganda Church. It was he more than any other who so implanted a living devotion to Christ in the African breast that within eight years of the advent of His Gospel Africans were prepared to die for Him.

It is desirable not to exaggerate the extent or the nature of these Uganda martyrdoms, but martyrdoms they were in the fullest sense of the word. Mwanga became kabaka on the death of his father in 1884. The years that ensued were a veritable age of Nero, and 1885 and 1886 were black with terror for the Christian adherents. Mackay writes on 25 May, 1886 :—

> What we have been in daily expectation of for a long time has now taken place—an order for the arrest of all the Christians. Eleven of our friends were thus killed the first day, and some of our old favourites condemned. May the Lord and Saviour Whom they have learned to trust be with the poor lads in this hour of horror and death, and give them a joyful entrance into the happy land. Armed bands were sent out in all directions and a host of our best people arrested, and an effort made to get them to inform on others. Even at Rusaka, the queen mother's place, many boys have been put to death. . . . The Lord mercifully look on the agony of these poor black children who are laying down their lives for His Name's sake.[1]

Two or three days after this the very flower of the Christian community, thirty-two in number, were slowly burnt to death, and that too by Mwanga's express orders.

[1] " The Story of Mackay of Uganda," pp. 280–2.

In a leading article dated 30 October, 1886, " The Times " affirmed :—

> The existence of the mission, lying altogether in Mwanga's power, yet staying against his declared will, is infinitely more conclusive evidence of the strength of Christianity in Africa than would be its predominance by the tyrant's dethronement. Its persistency is not merely magnanimous : it is the one way of testing the ability of Christian truth and humanity to hold its ground without the accessories of gunboats and rifles against both heathendom and Islam.

The simple words of Sir Henry Stanley are very touching :—

> God knows if ever man had reason to be doleful and lonely and sad, Mackay had when, after murdering his bishop, and burning his pupils, and strangling his converts, and clubbing to death his dark friends, Mwanga turned his eye of death on him. And yet the little man met it with calm blue eyes that never winked. To see one man of this kind, working day after day for twelve years bravely, and without a syllable of complaint or moan amid the wildernesses, and to hear him lead his little flock to show forth God's lovingkindness in the morning and His faithfulness every night, is worth going a long journey, for the moral courage and contentment that one derives from it.

It is impossible to overestimate the effect of such heroic endurance on the part of the early Uganda Church. Upon the Africans themselves the martyrdoms reacted with immediate force. The head executioner reported to the king that " he had never killed such brave people before ; that they died calling on God." Mackay, a little later, writes of " sitting up to all hours teaching housefuls." During the most dangerous period Baganda readers flocked to his house. The influence of such fortitude, however, did not end here. The martyrdoms naturally made an impression of the deepest kind, as " The Times " article indicates, in England. They arrested and modified public opinion with regard to the policy of native evangelization. They produced a certain something of religious seriousness and purpose which may be seen in the increased missionary activity in the Church, to be traced unquestionably to that remarkable decade (1880–90). In Uganda itself they laid the foundation of that Christian expansion which, as succeeding pages will show, has made the story of the last generation in Middle Africa without a parallel in the world.

I am far from suggesting that Mackay was solely responsible for this new temper of heroism in a race naturally so docile. Wilson, before Mackay arrived in 1878, was already teaching readers. In 1879, after the former's enforced withdrawal, Pearson was a devoted

Some Outstanding Memories

companion. All through 1880 Pearson was at Mackay's side. On 18 March, 1881, " a new era dawned on the mission with the arrival of the Rev. P. O'Flaherty." He stayed until 1885. In the month of May, 1883, the Rev. R. P. Ashe reached Uganda, " and Mackay soon recognized in him the same warmth of heart to the Lord Jesus, and the same burning zeal for missions, which had characterized his attached friend Dr. John Smith,"[1] who had died six years before. Ashe stayed in Uganda till 1886, and then Mackay was once more alone. The times were abnormally difficult. The conditions of life were daunting. The most fervent spirit might well have quailed in that jungle life, haunted with evil and treachery and cruelty. There is a touching note in 1879 : " There were thus seven C.M.S. missionaries in the country. With the exception of Mr. Pearson, however, they all soon left."[2] Matters were such just then that a complete withdrawal from Uganda was considered. The Roman Catholics did, in fact, withdraw for a time, 1882-85. This is only to disclose more evidently the plain fact that, amid much coming and going and under circumstances

[1] " The Story of Mackay of Uganda," p. 243.   [2] *Ibid.*, p. 145.

appalling to think of, this young Scots engineer in his thirties—in the face of all the Roman Catholic intrigues, in the face of all the vacillations of Mtesa, in the face of all the atrocities of Mwanga, including the murder in Busoga of the long-looked-for bishop—did quietly live on undismayed. And not only this. He lived on so openly and engagingly, and with so beautiful a spirit and so blameless an example—and all this in such nearness to the natives themselves—that, in doing so, he infected them with the contagious faith of his own life to such a degree that they were in a few short years prepared to die for the faith he thus inspired.

Mackay's gift to Uganda is thus, first and foremost, his joyous, infectious, unshakable faith in his ever-living, ever-present Redeemer. He left behind him two other legacies of priceless worth. From first to last he felt strongly that, for the Baganda, faith was meaningless without work. Their ingrained laziness stood between them and enlightenment. " He ever strove," says his biographer, " to instil into their minds by his own example the importance and dignity of labour, and that idleness is quite inconsistent with the Christian life."[1] A few

---
[1] " The Story of Mackay of Uganda," p. 299.

days before his death (8 February, 1890), he writes of his struggles with the rebuilding of his steamer : " I have been toiling at the forge and lathe and have got our steam arrangements far on to completion. The three-cylinder engine and two steam-pumps and injector stand all ready fitted for the boiler. The main boiler-shell is also carefully jointed and riveted together. . . . Many new parts had to be made and rivets also by the hundred. . . . High-pressure steam is not a thing to play with." So it was from the very beginning. " From his great skill in handicrafts, especially in all kinds of ironwork, Alexander Mackay soon became as much esteemed by King Mtesa and his court as the early smith was by our woad-stained ancestors." Mackay humorously styles himself as " engineer, builder, printer, physician, surgeon, and general artificer to Mtesa, Kabaka of Uganda, overlord of Unyoro, etc." Mackay is the Tubal Cain of Uganda. He is also its Caxton and its Tyndale.

A primitive people owes an inestimable debt to its first translators. Of such the roll in Uganda is a noble one. Pilkington and Rowling, Blackledge and Holden, Kitching and Willis, Lees and Dillistone have in different tribes and races been lasting benefactors. The long list must be headed by Mackay. His deft fingers, that at the age of 8 had first handled the type, were now to set it for the diffusion of the light amid the darkness of Africa. His musical ear was to catch the soft Luganda phrase and idiom and render into the speech of daily life the gospel story. In the Luganda Bible the whole of St. Matthew's Gospel and St. John's Gospel (chapters i-xiv) are an abiding possession from the pen of Mackay. To read Mackay's translation, especially of the parables, is to be listening to natives talking. It is characteristic of him that in the midst of the horrors of 1886 he quietly writes : " Praise God. St. Matthew's Gospel is now published complete in Luganda and rapidly being bought. I merely stitch it with title page and supply a loose cover." " I am plodding on, teaching, translating, printing, doctoring, and carpentering." That was just it—always plodding on, and because he did so the little Church in Uganda survived the storm.

III

While the patient endurance of Alexander Mackay was rekindling a fresh enthusiasm in the inner circle of the missionary-hearted,

Some Outstanding Memories 33

it was the dramatic death of Bishop Hannington that brought home the magnitude of the African venture to the Church at large. James Hannington went up to Oxford (St. Mary's Hall) in 1868 at the age of 21. Athlete and sportsman, with a keen love of adventure, he was already a natural leader. He had been destined by his father for a business career. Through the influence, however, of a saintly mother he was constrained to think rather of Holy Orders, and in 1874 he was ordained at Exeter to a curacy in a Devonshire parish. It was while at St. George's, Hurstpierpoint, that his spirit was stirred to the claims of service overseas. The deaths of Shergold Smith and O'Neill in 1878 had deeply affected him. On 29 November, 1881, the decision was made. " Went to Eastbourne," so runs his diary, " to a meeting of C.M.S. district secretaries. After lunch Mr. Eugene Stock spoke, clear and incisive. If he had asked me to go out I should have said : ' Yes ' ; I longed to offer myself to go." On 7 May, 1882, he sailed. With him in this new party were R. P. Ashe, then a Liverpool curate, J. Blackburn, W. J. Edmonds, E. C. Gordon from Islington, and C. Wise, an artisan. Of these Ashe alone reached Uganda. Hannington, prostrate with fever and dysentery, had to return home. But higher service was in store for him. For some years past the consecration of a Bishop for Eastern Equatorial Africa had been contemplated, first by Archbishop Tait, Henry Wright, and Bishop Steere of the U.M.C.A., next by Archbishop Benson, Bishop Smythies, and Mr. Wigram. James Hannington seemed clearly indicated for this great honour. He was now pronounced entirely fit. Dr. Benson accepted the suggestion. On St. John the Baptist's Day, 1884, Hannington was consecrated in Lambeth Parish Church.

The Bishop was destined never to reach Buganda. A year previously Joseph Thomson, on behalf of the Royal Geographical Society, had proved the practicability of a direct route from Mombasa to the north side of Lake Victoria. Hannington, in spite of ominous warnings, was attracted by this route, and, after many difficulties and certain thrilling adventures (his only travelling-companion, a native clergyman, William Jones, having been left with some of his men in Kavirondo), he at length reached Busoga on 21 October, 1885. Here, alarmed

Some Outstanding Memories 35

by the unprecedented advent of a white man by this northern route, the chief Luba detained him. On 29 October, after eight days of incredible suspense and misery, by Mwanga's orders he was put to death.

Many can still recall the immense impression created by this crime. If it was not for Hannington to benefit Uganda by his life, he was to serve her by his death. The assassination of a bishop—the first bishop of a new diocese—on the very threshold of his see, must in any event have arrested attention. Opinion, however, had already been stirred by Mwanga's atrocities. Hannington's little diary reached England by the same mail that brought news of the worst phase of the Uganda persecution. Here was a martyr Church, and a martyr bishop at its head. " Few events in our time," Dr. Eugene Stock rightly affirms, " have manifested more of the glory of God than the death of Bishop Hannington."

His death gave a new dignity in men's eyes to the missionary cause. In a leading article " The Times " (30 October, 1886), recalling the old saying that " the blood of the martyrs is the seed of the Church," declared that, "On the success of the Uganda experiment, with its alternation of favourable and adverse circumstances, depends the happiness of the interior of the vast continent for generations." Hannington's story, so admirably told by Canon E. C. Dawson, effected a revolution in regard to missionary literature. Far more than this, coming just when it did, Hannington's death helped to fan into a blaze that missionary flame that was so rapidly kindling in the Church. The year 1885 is memorable. That year the "Cambridge Seven," including the captain of the university eleven and the president of the University Boat Club, sailed for China. That year both the C.M.S. Clergy Union and the C.M.S. Ladies' Union were formed. The decade thus inaugurated witnessed a degree of personal response to the missionary call that is without parallel.

Two missionary parties that sailed during this period have left a permanent mark upon Uganda. The year 1887 saw D. Deekes, R. H. Walker, and Douglas Hooper travelling up-country under a new bishop, Henry Parker, together with Ashe and Blackburn, to join Mackay at Usambiro, by the southern shore of the Great Lake. Again the shepherd of the flock was taken. Again, as the news of Bishop Parker's death, and that of Blackburn, reached England, counsels of despair urged the abandonment of the mission. Again it was given to another of our younger clergy to save the day. R. H. Walker, fresh from his parish of All Souls, Langham Place, went to join Cyril Gordon in Uganda, and there, with the necessary furloughs, he toiled for twenty-five years, first as pioneer, then as administrator. He was the Barnabas of the mission, the encourager. As such his memory is fragrant still. In a dark hour he entered Uganda. By the sunshine of his spirit he cheered the fainting Church, and stood ready to usher in the new day that was soon to dawn with the coming of Bishop Tucker and many welcome recruits.

IV

Tucker, with Douglas Hooper, G. K. Baskerville, George Pilkington, J. W. Dunn, J. V. Dermott, F. C. Smith, and H. J. Hunt, reached the Great Lake in October, 1890. On St. Mark's Day, ten days after the sad telegram had told of Mackay's death, Alfred Tucker had been consecrated Bishop. In his "Eighteen Years in Uganda and East Africa" his graphic pen has set out for us a glowing picture of the great expansion that dates from his episcopate. When he arrived the number of baptized was about 200. When he left Uganda the total was 62,800. Native teachers at his coming there were none. At his departure they numbered over 2000. More than this, the little company that for fourteen years had centred at Namirembe had now become a great multitude among tribes and peoples far beyond the confines of Buganda. Ankole, Toro, Bunyoro, Patigo, Mbale, Busoga, Usukuma, Kavirondo figure in the statistics of 1907.

Circumstances of various kinds contributed to the bringing in of this brighter day. Bishop Tucker arrived on 27 December, 1890. On the very eve of his coming an event of enduring importance to Uganda had occurred. By some eight days he had been preceded by Captain Lugard, who, on behalf of the British East Africa Company, had presented to Mwanga and his chiefs a treaty for their signature. A document this with a story behind it. For the B.E.A. Company, not content with the development of the

Some Outstanding Memories 39

coast districts, had been energetic enough to dispatch two of its officials, Mr. Jackson and Mr. Gedge, to propose a similar treaty a year earlier, only to find themselves forestalled by one Karl Peters, a German agent, who, with the aid of the Roman mission, was seeking to keep the Company out. Events, however, had been moving fast elsewhere. Lord Salisbury, by the Anglo-German Agreement, had that same year secured Uganda definitely for British influence. Peters's schemes were thus foiled. Lugard's treaty was inevitably accepted. On 26 December Uganda came definitely under the protection of the British East Africa Company. In 1890, moreover, at the Brussels Conference the European Powers agreed to suppress the slave trade, and to prohibit the sale of strong spirits and fire-arms to Africans.

Politically, therefore, it was upon a new Uganda that in this year 1890 Tucker first set foot. Socially, too, the atmosphere was changed. Let the Bishop himself describe his first impressions : " Early in the morning after my arrival I was roused from my slumbers by a murmur of voices. It seemed as though a continuous stream of people was flowing past the house. . . . It was a remarkable sight that met my gaze as I entered the church. . . . Here on my right hand was Apolo Kagwa, the Katikiro, a baptized Christian. There were Sembera Mackay and Henry Wright Duta, and in front a great crowd of apparently earnest worshippers. Some thousand souls were gathered together inside the church and outside, about the doors and windows. The whole assembly seemed to be pervaded with a spirit of earnest devotion." There is in all this a freedom from the former terror. Mwanga is curbed. The fear of the white man is gone. There is the evident beginning here of the Uganda we know to-day. On a large scale there is the desire to learn. The leaven of the mass movement is at work.

Under such altered conditions Tucker and his able lieutenants delightedly toiled. The Bishop in all his eighteen years never acquired the language. In consequence he never entered into conversation with a native. He never knew the native mind. His artistic spirit revelled in the scenic effect of these primitive congregations. His eager, affectionate nature read into them much that was not there. His geese were often swans. Much therefore of his ecclesiastical adaptation was premature. He mistook docility for stability. The child he treated as an adult, not least in regard to the native ministry.

Make, however, what reservations you may, Tucker was a great administrator. With a British instinct for government, he harnessed whatever was suitable in native custom to the service of the Church. Always the father, he was a true bishop. As bishop, too, he was invariably the champion of his flock, the staunch upholder of their rights. In return the people revered him. With quick responsiveness they carried out his designs, and that these designs so amazingly prospered is because through everything Tucker was pre-eminently the Christian. The love of Christ constrained him. The desire to bring his people to Christ was his passion. The mission around him, whatever his mistakes, grew up in a world of zeal and prayer.

So it was that amid much external unrest, due to Mwanga's ceaseless intrigues with Arabs, Sudanese, and the conflicting factions at Mengo, the early 'nineties proved to be the golden age of the Uganda Mission. It was a time of strong and ever stronger reinforcements. On his first return Bishop Tucker had asked for forty new men. Before 1894 forty new workers did actually sail for Eastern Equatorial Africa.[1] These included E. H. Hubbard, W. A. Crabtree, A. B. Fisher, R. H. Leakey, E. Millar, F. Rowling, T. B. Fletcher, H. R. Sugden, H. B. Lewin, A. B. Lloyd, A. J. Pike, G. R. Blackledge— a remarkable body of men who have been truly pillars of the Uganda Church and who have carried the Gospel from Uganda north and south and east and west.

During this time, too, came that crisis when, largely through the Bishop's exertions, Uganda was retained within British influence. In 1891 the British East Africa Company, disappointed at the Government's failure to provide a railway, and unable to continue unaided the immense expenditure of occupying Uganda,[2] resolved to withdraw. Sir William Mackinnon, the chairman, met the Bishop by accident in Scotland. Could the C.M.S. help to save the situation ? he asked. Could the C.M.S. give £15,000 ? No, was the unhesitating answer. Then on 30 October

[1] "History of the C.M.S.," Vol. III, p. 458.
[2] Then £40,000 a year.

Some Outstanding Memories 43

came the Gleaners' Union Anniversary, and Tucker's passionate appeal. The remarkable result is known. The money was contributed. The order for withdrawal was cancelled. Uganda for the time being was safe. Public opinion meanwhile had been deeply stirred; and when in 1892 Mr. Gladstone's ministry entered office, and the B.E.A. Company again gave notice of withdrawal, Lord Rosebery as Foreign Secretary stoutly championed the retention of Uganda. Sir Gerald Portal was sent as a special commissioner to Uganda to report on the best means of dealing with the country. He arrived in March, 1893, and on 1 April, at the Fort of Kampala, in a setting of much impressiveness, the company's flag having been lowered, the British flag was unfurled in its stead. Sir Gerald in his report strongly recommended the establishment of a British Protectorate in Uganda and the construction of a railway from the coast. The Protectorate was voted in the House of Commons on 1 June, 1894, and the railway, on the proposal of Sir Edward Grey, on 13 June, 1895. Colonel Colville became first Commissioner in 1893, and from that time onward Government and missions have developed the country in closest accord.

Something more, however, than either strong reinforcements or settled administration is needed to account for the spring and buoyancy of those memorable years. Let one of those who had newly arrived describe it in his own words: " Perhaps it is well-nigh impossible for a Christian worker in England to understand what an overwhelming joy it was to the pioneer missionary of those days to see the all-conquering power of the Word of God." Bishop Tucker tells of the growing Church, of the first Confirmation, the first appointment of lay teachers, and the first ordination. It is evident that the moving power was the first, fresh impact of the New Testament writings upon the people in their own homely tongue. Gordon and Ashe had continued Mackay's translation of the gospels. It was left for George Pilkington, the Cambridge classical scholar and Harrow master, to complete the New Testament and to translate most of the Old Testament as well. So eager was the demand that, on the arrival of the first consignment from England, 660 books were sold daily for eleven days. Revival followed —a real revival through the reception of the Holy Spirit that profoundly touched and re-inspired the Church. And from

Some Outstanding Memories 45

that time dates the great expansion of which succeeding chapters will tell. Well may it have been " an overwhelming joy " to be a pioneer missionary in those days.

CHAPTER III

TRANSFORMATION

MR. WINSTON CHURCHILL, in his volume entitled "My African Journey," borrows from the familiar nursery story an arresting figure. Instead of a beanstalk, he says, you climb up a railway; but it is to find the same fairyland at the top. Of the fairyland we shall speak later. The remarkable stairway by which you ascend to it first claims attention. For if any saving instrument of man's device has brought redemption to a beleaguered people it is the Uganda Railway. No record of the Uganda Mission should fail to pay tribute to those indomitable engineers by whose genius the horrors of the first marches into the interior of Africa have been transformed into the ease and fascination of modern travel.

R. W. Emerson once declared that "when the Indian trail gets widened, graded, and bridged to a good road, there is a benefactor, there is a missionary, a pacificator, a wealth-bringer, a maker of markets, a vent for industry." Writing so early as 4 June,

Transformation

1878, Alexander Mackay affirmed: "One thing is certain: this land will ever remain little else than what it is—dark, benighted Africa—until we can find some easy means of travel and transit in it. Very few could endure the trials and hardships we went through in the early months of this year." Before Mackay's death in 1890 his views about a railway of very light construction were assented to by H. M. Stanley, who promised to do all in his power to persuade Sir William Mackinnon, of the British East Africa Company, of the necessity for it. Of those first journeys into the interior one can scarcely read without a shudder. Between the experiences so vividly narrated by Mackay in 1876, or by the Rev. R. P. Ashe in 1882—and even those described by Bishop Tucker or the Rev. J. B. Purvis in the 'nineties —there is an appreciable difference. Upon that wearisome southern route from Zanzibar, by Mpwapwa, Ugogo, and Unyamwezi, the ordeals of desertion, robbers, malaria, shortage of food and water follow on one another in a sickening succession. The marvel is that Uganda ever was reached in the 'seventies.

Now, from Mombasa on the Indian Ocean to Kisumu on Lake Victoria, along an unbroken track of 585 miles, runs the Uganda Railway. Mombasa is one white glare with patches of glorious colour at many a corner. The old Portuguese Fort of Jesus gives it a touch of antiquity and of history rare in East Africa. The red flag of the Sultan of Zanzibar shows that he is still landlord; but the sunset bugle each night at 6 p.m., as his flag is lowered, has a British note; and H.M. High Court of East Africa, with bougainvillæa and palm in the foreground, stands near by. The fort, the flag, the law court in one glance offer to you the outline of the island's history; the touch of blue water below the fort, called Mombasa harbour, to the north, and Kilindini to the south of the island (for Mombasa is surrounded by water) point to its strategic importance on the east coast of Africa. Another vista, comprising Mombasa Cathedral, with its dome and cross, and the statue of Sir William Mackinnon, completes the picture. But to the station and the Nairobi express.

No traveller, however blasé, can resist some exuberance over this amazing line. Where a generation past tramped Tucker and Baskerville, Pilkington and Millar, Wilson and Lloyd, and even the intrepid women in 1895, you now speed in a comfortable saloon, three kinds of window (smoked glass, louvre, and gauze) vying with one another for your convenience. Up and up by windings through the hills, then on and on over the vast, tawny expanses of the Kapiti and the Athi plains, powdered at night by the red sand, breaking your fast by day at well-found refreshment " halts," you accomplish in two days what your predecessors could barely do in two months. The lion and rhinoceros are now rarely seen from the train, but the giraffe, the zebra, the ostrich, the buffalo, and many kinds of antelope are still found alongside the track.

Half-way comes Nairobi, at the foot of the highlands, in itself a succession of surprises. How staggered would Mackay be with the broad platforms of Nairobi station, and its yet broader streets, its race-course and polo-ground, its villas, its hotels, its clubs. Then above Nairobi, amid the famed highlands of Kenya, 7000 feet high and more, comes the journey's special thrill. Across this high plateau cleft in the earth's crust, like a crack in some well-baked cake, runs that unique geological formation, the Rift Valley. Beginning below the Sea of Galilee, striking south in a single, unbroken crevasse through the Dead Sea and the Gulf of Akaba and the Red Sea and Lake Rudolf, runs this cleavage in the earth's surface, like to nothing save a similar valley in the moon. First up and over one wall of it, then up and over the next climbs this undaunted train. The night as you cross the Mau summit is bitterly cold. This African railway-night has a quality of its own. On and upward crawls the train, into deep gullies and gorges rendered mysterious by the darkness. At times you see just enough to seem suspended over a fathomless abyss. Later the moon rises and gives you the impression of wandering in some astral crater. Then with the dawn of day the ridge is past, and by corresponding gradients and monster curves you speed downward till the Great Lake is reached.

Another jubilee contrast. Mr. Purvis is nowhere happier in his graphic volume, "Through Uganda to Mount Elgon," than where he enlarges upon the canoe of a generation ago. " The traveller is naturally interested in the vessel that carries him, and he is considerably disconcerted to learn in the first place that it literally hangs together by a mere thread. . . . The boards are thinned and bent and sewn together with the

Transformation 51

fibre of a palm tree . . . which has been known to give way and allow the keelboard to drop out at an inconvenient distance from the shore."[1] But what took Mr. Purvis, as he tells us, six days to accomplish is now done from Kisumu to Entebbe in some eighteen to twenty hours, while for his frail and primitive canoe you are now offered the white decks and the gleaming brass-work of the " Clement Hill," a vessel of graceful lines that after many years still adorns the navy of the Colonial Office. So by these gracious means is the traveller to-day deposited at the very centre of the African continent. With what exactitude has been conceded Mackay's demand for " the only power which will ever effectually bring the light of civilization into the heart of Africa—the iron horse."

With this transformation of the avenue of approach the last half-century has witnessed in the heart of Africa a yet more arresting change. If the traveller is as a rule quite unprepared for the wonder of the Uganda Railway, he is equally surprised by the wonder of the Uganda roads, and what they disclose on either side.

Entebbe, where you first set foot in

[1] P. 97.

Uganda, is, of course, a thing apart. Entebbe fifty years ago was but the obvious landing-place from the Great Lake. Ashe writes of his arrival : " Making our way along by the archipelago of the Sese Islands, we finally landed at a place called Entebbe, about thirty miles from Mtesa's lubiri or capital." Entebbe to-day, in part by its natural features, in part by the stringent clearing of bush and scrub in the fight against the tsetse-fly and the mosquito, yet much more by the British genius for order and beauty, is a gem among government head-quarters. As Cap Martin, hot and wooded, protrudes into the blue waters of the Mediterranean, so with just the Riviera charm of sunshine and tone, with its wealth of stately trees and cosy bungalows, does Entebbe stand out into the glistening sheet of Lake Victoria—the red roads and vivid green slopes picked out with the frequent purple of bougainvillæa and the pale pink of oleander, giving it a perpetual joyousness of colour. Here in the rank untidiness of Africa is an exquisite oasis of order, a tribute to the Union Jack hanging limply from the flagstaff of Government House on the crest of the hill.

Yet even as you leave Entebbe and commit

yourself to the interest of the road to Kampala, where else, you may well ask yourself, could your motor find a finer surface, a better camber, easier gradients, or wider curves? The metalled roads of Uganda, owing to a conglomerate called *murram* (a species of glutinous gravel found almost ubiquitously in the Protectorate), are famous through Africa, and speak volumes for the native skill that goes to their making. West and south-west and north-east for hundreds of miles go these roads from Kampala, linking Uganda with Kenya and Ruanda, with the Belgian Congo and the Sudan; and offering transport for the produce that constitutes a growing export trade. There is a modesty in the African landscape that veils her best features from the passer-by; and little do you see from the road of her domesticities or of her culture. When, however, you realize that the exports of cotton, coffee, ground nuts, simsim, sesame, rubber, hides, skins, and other produce reached the value of over £5,000,000 in 1925, you have cause to appreciate the diligence of the native in regions that fifty years ago seemed so unhopeful. Once again the wilderness and the solitary place are glad and the desert is blossoming as the rose.

How has all this come about? Whence has sprung this regenerated earth? It is because the people themselves have realized their true capacity to be partners with civilized men in the production of their country's richness. It is because they have imbibed, even if only partially, the knowledge of that fuller life which Christianity imparts. The real transformation of Uganda has been the transformation of its people.

To approach Kampala on the Entebbe road is to become conscious several miles away, first at one bend of the road, then at another, of one feature dominating the whole landscape: of the seven hills of which Kampala is composed, one, called Namirembe, by its detached position, by its clear-cut outline, commands a certain homage of its own. To reflect upon its story is to see how justly such homage is deserved. Not once nor twice in the story of nations has the sentiment of a whole people centred in some historic hill. What the Hill of Sion was to the Hebrew race, what the Acropolis was to the Athenian, what the Capitol was to the republic of Rome, what the Castle Rock has been to the Scot, or the Kremlin to the Russian people, even such has been Namirembe in the story of Uganda. The record of these fifty years stands graven upon its summit and its slopes. Picture then, as your motor glides so easily at its base, something of the then and the now. " We feel sorely downcast," writes Mackay on Christmas Eve, 1880. " Our last hopes seem gone. The lads who had learnt the most and seemed most impressed have been put out of the way. Others who have been taught more or less are afraid to come to us any more. The few chiefs of whom we had hopes have gone back, while other chiefs and the king (Mtesa) seem daily to become more hardened and hopelessly sunk in every form of vice and villainy." There yonder to the left of the hill, at Natete, where every year on November 29, the Commemoration of the Martyrs is still held, we picture Mackay, sometimes quite alone, sometimes with Pearson or O'Flaherty, sometimes with Ashe, holding on, cast down but not destroyed, perplexed but not in despair, in the face of what seemed insuperable odds : begging of Mtesa a small plot on which to grow food, begging to be allowed to teach.

And now !

Look to the crest of that hill. There, high above you, its light-coloured brick often gleaming golden in the evening light, rises

Namirembe Cathedral, every part of it an answer to Mackay's challenge that same Christmas Eve, " Is anything too hard for the Lord ? " " The present deathblow to the Christian Creed " he foresaw to be " only the prelude to its glorious resurrection."

By what heroic stages that cathedral has risen ! In the darkest hour of Mwanga's persecutions it is on record that on 26 July, 1885, a congregation of 175 gathered at the mission house for prayer, and thirty-five partook of the Holy Communion. The Church " in the house " here, as in Ephesus or Corinth in the early days, is the first " ecclesia." Next—not on the summit, but on the lower slopes—when the fire of persecution was past, the first church in Uganda was planted. Of that memorable event the Rev. R. H. (afterwards Archdeacon) Walker wrote in March, 1890 : " In the heart of the dark continent a native building is being erected for the sole use of worshipping God." Third in the sequence, amid much rejoicing, the first church on the summit of the hill was opened on 31 July, 1892—to be destroyed by a violent tropical storm two years later. It speaks volumes for African enthusiasm that by 1895 yet another church

THE MISSION BUILDINGS ON NAMIREMBE HILL

A rough sketch to indicate (1) St. Paul's Cathedral. (2) Chapter Room. (3) House of Archdeacon Blackledge. (4) The Kabaka's lubiri (on hill opposite). (5) Road from Kampala. (6) Schoolhouse of Mengo High School. (7) Native clergyman's house. (8) Old Lychgate of former Cathedral. (9) Hill-side whereon are the Mengo Hospital and several missionaries' houses. (10) Procession of boys from Mengo Central School, ascending to the Cathedral. (11) Tennis courts. (12) Drive to Bishop's House.

was reared, this time to be the cathedral of Uganda. Some stirring years of progress it witnessed. But a more permanent edifice was desired, and under the direction of Mr. K. E. Borup the first brick building was raised and consecrated by Bishop Tucker on 21 June, 1904. Six years and this second cathedral was also destroyed, by fire. It was only at the close of the war in 1919 that by strenuous effort, largely inspired by Canon Rowling, the present cathedral was completed from designs by Professor Beresford Pite. It stands a monument to native generosity and missionary perseverance, its mighty walls, its supporting buttresses, and its well-built keystones calculated to endure for long years the assaults of time and storm.

Namirembe as it is to-day, its flanks now clothed with many a shapely bungalow or hospital building, its shoulders encircled with diocesan halls or schools, and, high above all, the dome of this new St. Paul's Cathedral surmounted by the Cross, presents a succession of scenes that vividly testify to the amazing transformation that the last fifty years have witnessed. The cathedral itself naturally takes first place. It is the occasion of the Synod; and now, in triumphant contrast to the horrors of Mwanga's reign, only forty years gone by, see the Church that out of those martyr fires has sprung into life. Two and two in a long line come the clergy white and black, in order of seniority, irrespective of race. No hasty ordination here. Through long stages of preparation—first as lay readers, then as deacons, with intervals of college life alternating with responsible pastoral work— these black clergy (now seventy-one in number) have attained to the ministry of Christ's Church. In front are middle-aged men, some now representing the outlying districts; behind the seniors—Yonasani Kaidzi, ordained so long ago as 1893; Canon Mudeka, senior native clergyman; Tomasi Senfuma, taught by Mackay; Apolo Kivebulaya of the pygmy forest. Interspersed with them are their brethren who for long years have built them up in the faith, Blackledge and Ladbury, Weatherhead, Leakey, and Wilson, Daniell and Gill, Garrett and Mathers, Lewin and Lloyd, and numbers more. Last of all comes the Bishop. And as they enter by the west door see from what distant regions the lay members of the Synod are convened. Here are brethren from far off Gulu, adjacent to the Sudan, from the mountain ridges of Elgon, from the plains of Teso, from Toro, Bunyoro, Ankole, and even Ruanda : " Out of every nation and kindred and people." As the Church in England welded the heptarchy into one nation, so in the Protectorate of Uganda men who never before met in peaceful guise can now through the same influence sit in Christian fraternity.[1]

If our first scene presents the Uganda Church in worship, the second must show its leaders in council. If the one displays the product, the other reveals something of the process. Come half a dozen steps down from the south transept of the cathedral and enter the chapter-house. Looking down upon you from the walls are portraits of the men who have gone on before. Here are Tucker and Hannington, Millar and Pilkington, and many more. Here is the Lambeth group of 1920, to remind the Uganda Diocesan Council of their integral part in the Anglican Church. More striking still are the living figures. For membership in the Diocesan Council is an honour coveted by chiefs and clergy alike. Fortnightly it meets. Fortnightly the whole orbit of the diocese comes up for circumspection. Is it the

[1] The memory is of 1921.

minutes of some remote deanery? All minutes from outlying rural deaneries must be ratified by the Diocesan Council before they can take effect. Is it some case of discipline or of church order? Mark the care with which all is conducted. Mark the voting. Archbishop Temple quotes a Frenchman who declared that British votes are generally seven to six. This kind of vote would often obtain in Uganda, but once the vote is taken the decision of the majority is law. The Baganda are temperamentally constitutional.

But who are these on the other face of the hill, who, hundred upon hundred, in their white *kanzus*, are ascending, like some snowy escalator, to the cathedral door? The basis of all church life in Uganda is the school. These 600 white-robed figures are the boys of Mengo Central School. They speak much for the boy life of the district. They speak more for their head-master, the Rev. Fesito Luboyera. Come down some morning past the Bishop's house to the slope of the hill on which the school is built. Class-room after class-room is packed with keen, eager faces. You are prepared it may be to take the top Form (Standard VII) in English. " The World We Live In " is the book they are reading; and, as the boys read to you or answer questions about Manchester trade or university education, it is to show you how quick is their grasp and how eager their desire for cosmopolitan information. The head-master's time-table is adhered to with precision. Woe betide you if you arrive late for your lesson! School or play or religion, it is all one with this most gentle and most effective Fesito. Your steps take you perchance that way at that perfect hour of the tropical day from 5 to 6 p.m. Here is Fesito upon the football field, teaching the boys to play the game as he in turn has learnt it from a member of a college team at Cambridge. Talk to Fesito again about his boys and their personal life. He believes in regular Communion for those confirmed, but no Communion will he sanction without preparation. To minister the Sacrament to his boys at the cathedral rail is to be aware how well that preparation has been given. It is the personal influence of this man that accounts for the presence of these white-robed day-boys, who each Sunday fill the large south transept. On week-days khaki shirt and shorts are now the rule. To meet these boys—trim, athletic-looking, and cheerful—swarming up by the hundred each

Transformation 63

morning to the school, and to reflect upon things as they were a short generation ago, is indeed to thank God and take courage.

What of the homes of these boys ? Where do they come from ? You may well ask. To look out from the high plateau of the cathedral is to see indeed certain outstanding edifices. Down beyond the cincture of mission buildings are the shops of the Mengo market ; and opposite, on Mengo Hill, is that stockade of the lubiri, that from the days of Mackay and Ashe has figured in every Uganda story. Homes, too, of the great chiefs emerge, and round to the east lie the Indian quarter on Nakasero, with the British bungalows above. Even here at the capital, as elsewhere in Uganda, all is green. On every side, bright aurelian to deep emerald, are the swaying leaves of the banana, hiding every vestige of humanity. There is always a mystery as to where and how the people live ; and this element of mystery does not end when, threading your way by the little devious paths in and out of the banana-stems, you try to visit them in their homes. Have they homes as yet ? Now and again some special invitation is sent. I well remember one such, from the wife of a leading chief. Who that has assisted at a native feast can forget the care with which each ceremony is performed—the handwashing, the unfolding of the steaming basket of plantains, the gentle kneading of one's portion, and the vain effort to enjoy it? What I prefer to recall is the simple dignity of that home and all the courtesy and the kindliness that went to make our visit memorable. Here were father and mother, both Christians of long standing and high character. Here, at all events, was a Christian family.

Where religion can produce such a home as this the foundations of a people's life have been well and truly laid. We discussed this idea of family life once with the Kabaka himself, H.H. Daudi Chwa. He and his wife (Irene) were our guests at tea. The conversation turned on the supposed absence of a word for "family" in the Luganda speech. *Kika* we knew, the word for clan. "Yes," said the Kabaka, "and for 'family' we have the word *enda*." "But is it in the Bible?" We tried the obvious places: "Every family in heaven and earth" (Eph. iii. 15) *buli kika*; "All families in heaven and earth" (Gen. xii. 3) again *ebika byona*. But the Kabaka persisted:

"It is in the Bible," he said. And, sure enough, some three hours later came this note by special messenger from the lubiri :

"The word (*enda*) is in Okubala, viz., Numbers xxvi. 5 and 12 and 15, and it is written 'family' in English.
"Yours sincerely,
"DAUDI CHWA, 15-4-21."

There is no such thing as a concordance in Luganda! I cherish the Kabaka's note, not merely as a token of his intimacy with the Scriptures, but as some indication of the pride he and his people already take in the family idea and of their desire to foster the conception of a home.

Against the backwardness, the cruelty, the horror of a past which is only fifty years distant Namirembe stands up before you as a witness to what the divine Spirit can achieve through a living Church, a Christian education, a Christian home-life. But before you pass from the hill there is something still to show you of Christianity in action which will perhaps demonstrate yet more visibly to the actual eye the sort of transformation I am trying to convey.

Down the ages tropical Africa has had

certain relentless foes to fight—slavery, witchcraft, cruelty, land-spoliation, and disease. It may be questioned whether disease, with its havoc and its degradation, is not the worst of all. Even to-day, such are the ravages of insects, vermin, heredity, and lust in certain districts that plague, malaria, and sleeping sickness are constantly recurring. Venereal disease most of all is always present. In his evidence before Sir Robert Coryndon's Commission upon the welfare of the Uganda Protectorate, Dr. Albert Cook stated that through this one disease sixty-seven per cent of the babies in Uganda die pre-natally, and that of those that are born only one in three comes to maturity. Until the launching of the recent medical campaign this disease threatened to obliterate whole portions of the already sparse population.

To look out upon Namirembe Hill from the opposing heights of Rubaga is to see at one glance how much of this central stronghold of Christianity is devoted to the ministry of healing. Bishop Tucker speaks of the joy with which, on 1 October, 1896, he welcomed at Mombasa Callis, Dr. A. R. Cook, Wigram, Clayton, Weatherhead, Tegart, Whitehouse, Miss Taylor, and Miss

Timpson (afterwards Mrs. A. R. Cook), all out for the first time. Medical work could now begin in earnest. " The organization of this much needed development of our missionary work," says the Bishop, " was at once entered upon with all his characteristic energy by Dr. A. R. Cook ; and in the month of June a mission hospital, built by the natives themselves, was opened and solemnly dedicated by prayer to the service of God." In the same month, therefore, in which the Mission celebrates its jubilee Mengo Hospital, that has played so vital a part in the life of the Mission, completes its generation. For thirty years Dr. and Mrs. Albert Cook have by their combined genius and devotion fostered stage by stage this amazing African achievement.

In 1897 Mengo Hospital, so we gather, was a grass hut standing upon something of a clearing on the hillside. Enter it to-day. Could any transformation be more complete ? Over the central sloping lawn towers the giant white flagstaff. In the main block is the doctor's consulting room. Medical works of every kind line the walls. His operating theatre and his X-ray theatre are replete with every accessory. Right and left stretch the native wards, the beds labelled above with familiar names of the English parishes or friends that support them. Here are native patients from far and wide. Outside, to the right, is the trim bungalow hospital for Europeans. I remember one afternoon finding herein a planter from Toro who had been gnawed by a lion, another man with gland trouble from far-off Tanganyika, and the wife of a government official from Nairobi. From all parts of East Africa they come. Completing the ellipse are the Indian ward and the dispensary, with its daily stream of out-patients.

An oasis this of peace and healing, friendliness and sunshine. What the doctors and nurses have accomplished under God in the fighting of disease and the assuaging of pain, in the healing of the tired body and the binding up of the broken-hearted, no human record can show. If you would in any degree attempt to appraise the coming of Christ to Uganda you must mark His handiwork in Mengo Hospital.

CHAPTER IV

EXPANSION WESTWARD

AT the entrance to Mombasa harbour, upon the palm-clad headland opposite the old custom house, you may see a solitary grave. The brief epitaph runs : " In memory of Mrs. L. Krapf, wife of the Rev. Dr. Krapf, Missionary of the Church of England, 13 July, 1844." What gives to this quiet resting-place its significance is the message that the husband sent home to England : " Tell your friends that on the east coast of Africa there is a lonely grave—a token that we have taken possession of the land for Christ. As in warfare, victory is often won by stepping over the graves of those who have gone before. Take this as a sign that you are called to the conquest of this continent for Christ, beginning at the eastern shore." As I stood by the grave I could not but cast my mind over the long chain of Christian outposts that my own eyes had seen stretching westward from Mombasa through Kenya and Uganda, and right on through Toro into the Congo Belge. I felt how far beyond all

MAP OF THE UGANDA PROTECTORATE

Showing means of communication by rail, road, river, and lake. The projected extension of the Uganda Railway from Tororo to Jinja is shown by the dotted line.

Expansion Westward

that he could have asked or thought the conquest for which Krapf prayed had already been achieved. This chapter traces in outline this onward march of the Church to the west.

It was in the spring of 1896 that Bishop Tucker set out formally to inaugurate work in Toro. From Kampala the distance to Toro is just 200 miles. It took the Bishop and his party a month to do the journey on foot. It may now be done by motor in a day. How had Christianity found its way to Toro? Let Bishop Tucker answer in his own words :—

It was in this wise. Yafeti Byakweyamba, a cousin of Kasagama, King of Toro, and a prince of the house of Kabarega, King of Bunyoro, had been brought up in Uganda, converted and baptized there. On becoming chief of Mwenge, a county of Toro, he asked that Christian teachers might be sent from Mengo to instruct his people. This was done, and two men, Marko and Petero, were sent as the two first missionary evangelists to the Batoro. In 1891 Kasagama was appointed by Captain Lugard the overlord of the Toro confederacy—in other words, " King " of Toro. He was a reader, but not baptized until his journey to Mengo at the close of 1895 brought him under regular Christian instruction. This event, so fraught with momentous consequences to the future of Toro, took place on 15 March, 1896. Thus it came about, in the good providence of God, that on our arrival on 30 April, 1896, we found ourselves face to face with an incipient Christianity.

How does it fare with Toro to-day after thirty years? Toro is a little world of its own. It is one of the *culs-de-sac* of the British Empire. It is the end of the road. It is the extreme western point of East Africa and of the Uganda Protectorate. Here you come up against the massive wall of Ruwenzori, which with the Semliki River and Lake Albert makes the frontier-line between ourselves and the Belgians in their immense Congo domain. Fort Portal (so called after Sir Gerald Portal) is the administrative centre of British rule, as Kabarole, the *mukama's* (presiding chief) hill, is of the native regime.

To come into Toro is to come over a high pass (Butiti) into a great basin among the hills. Ruwenzori, the range of the Mountains of the Moon, is 17,000 feet high, 2000 feet higher than Mont Blanc. It takes five whole days to reach its summit. The climate of Toro is very agreeable. The same height as Nairobi, you are never too hot and never too cold. No mosquitoes are here. Neither glass nor gauze fills your window-frames. Shutters there are to keep out lions and other

Expansion Westward 73

intruders at night. As in England, you sleep with two blankets, and you can wear a tweed coat after 4 p.m.

There are three centres of activity on the three adjacent hills. First and foremost is the round green hill of Fort Portal, the old fort of Captain Lugard still showing at its centre. At the end of your long 200-mile run you come on it as an oasis of neatness and kindliness and strength in a waste land. It is England in the heart of Africa. It is British occupation at its irreducible minimum. As it is typical of so many more government stations in Middle Africa it is worth careful attention. Central on a spacious lawn floats the Union Jack. Close by stands the black sentry, smartness itself in his khaki tunic and shorts, his scarlet cummerbund and his blue puttees. On either side of this village green the neat bungalows of the officials snuggle among roses and oleander. Everywhere—most British of all things—are trim hedges. Yonder, of course, is the tennis court, and on the glacis of the green hill, equally a matter of course, are the golf links. Here on this compact little emerald isle live the nine young Englishmen who rule and discipline and judge and develop this western province of the Uganda Protectorate : the

F

commissioners, the police officer, the roadmaker (P.W.D.), the agriculturist, etc. To have tea on his veranda with one of these is to feel for the moment out of Africa and at home.

Cross the bridge, climb up beyond it, and you are on a steep ascent to the citadel of the Mukama—a succession of little courts and guard-huts leading to the domicile within. To the artistic mind of Bishop Tucker this Mukama was always " King " of Toro. To our administration at Fort Portal he is the presiding chief of the district. King, Mukama, or chief, he is an attractive young fellow, with an estimable wife. He speaks some English, but there is something pathetic about the bareness of their life. Escaped from savagery and heathenism, they still seem unable to enter the fields of education and the higher interests of life.

Between these two powers that be, midway between these two centres of authority— British and native—and, as I feel, uniting them both, is the third hill. Here a well-planned array of buildings—religious, medical, educational, and domestic—set out the enterprise of the Christian Church. After Namirembe, Kabarole is one of the best

Expansion Westward

equipped of our stations. A mission station can never look very trim. It cannot show the well-groomed appearance of the administrative station, for the simple reason that church, hospital, and school must always be half buried by the banana groves upon which the native clergy, medical attendants, and teachers must live. But, accepting the banana tree, Kabarole is a fine station. First, and rightly, you come on the hospital designed by the Rev. H. E. Maddox, architect as well as clergyman. The hospital has been chiefly the product of the creative spirit of Dr. and Mrs. Ashton Bond. To pass along the wards, and to join the doctor in the simple morning prayers, is to realize the immeasurable blessing of this hospital upon the remotest flank of our Empire. An aged chief in a private ward to whom I spoke a few words, replied to me: " I put my faith in God and the doctor."

Toro has been equally blessed in its spiritual heads—Fisher, Kitching, Tegart, Blackledge, Russell, and Lloyd. The mission has now completed a generation of Christian service. How do things stand? At this frontier outpost the spiritual battle has swayed this way and that and there have been many adversaries. I can only record what I have seen myself. It was the Christmas of 1920 that I was privileged to spend there. Would that many in England could have shared my experience. On Christmas Eve (for a preparation service), on Christmas Day (for the Holy Communion), on St. Stephen's Day (for the Confirmation), the church was packed. It is a beautiful church, designed and built by the same missionary architect who designed the hospital. Bishop Tucker eloquently writes of his first visit to Toro in 1896 : tells of Kasagama, its young king ; of the Queen Mother and of the Queen, whom he himself baptized respectively Victoria and Damaris. Well, after a quarter of a century here they all were still, these three the first to come up to the Communion rail on Christmas Day—Kasagama at the south end, the two ladies at the north end. As I was at the north side, Victoria and Damaris were the two first Toro Christians to whom I administered the Holy Communion. A great privilege I felt it to be. What a noble constancy has been theirs ! On Christmas Day the stream of communicants was remarkable. About 400 came in all. For the first time in Uganda I was struck by the faces of the women. The

Expansion Westward

Queen, who has an attractive face, is a great worker, and prepares women for Confirmation. She has learnt weaving at our mission looms. The women of Toro, thanks to the devoted teaching of certain outstanding women missionaries, are distinctly ahead of the women of Uganda.

It is this evidence of what Christianity can be and do in a country like Toro that fills one with anguish at the shortage of men and women to give the needed lead. The Church is passing through a period of sore trial. Venereal disease is working havoc in the land. Kasagama himself, with all his public spirit, has felt, like so many African chiefs, the dominating pressure of earlier habits and inheritances. He knows it is the same with his people. "My people," he said sadly, "are getting cold. We want more European missionaries." The Batoro are children still. They must for many years to come be led by the hand. Their very readiness to be guided casts on the Church greater responsibility.

There is a further reason why this Toro mission is so strategically outstanding, and why in this record it should receive special place. I have spoken of Toro as a *cul-de-sac*, and of the mighty rampart of

Ruwenzori as a bar to further advance towards the west. So it might have been to European conceptions; but not to the grace of God, not to the onward urge of His Spirit, not to the evangelistic zeal of the African himself. The romantic story of the Mboga mission, and of its founder, Apolo Kivebulaya, is proof that in Africa the Gospel of Christ is to know no limits.

The sketch of this "Apolo of the Pygmy Forest," from the graphic pen of Archdeacon Lloyd, has already come to the hands of so many who may see these pages that the present summary must be concise. Born of poor parents about the year 1864, Apolo spent his early years among the darkest heathen surroundings; and yet for the past thirty years (as the Archdeacon affirms) he has been a light-bearer to some of the most degraded tribes in Africa. The child of a Mohammedan, it was under Moslem influences that he seemed destined to live. But God ordered otherwise. As a boy of 13 Apolo remembers the advent of two white men;[1] and, after initial suspicions, Mtesa's counsel to his people to adhere to these new teachers. It was after Mtesa's death, during Mwanga's persecutions, that Apolo

[1] Shergold Smith and Wilson in 1877.

Expansion Westward 79

first came to Mengo. Through the chance word of a friend he was led to the presence of the great Alexander Mackay, who in loneliness was facing the fury of the Kabaka. Even then Mackay was at work on translation, and this African boy learnt much from him. He learnt especially that which Mackay could give him best of all, until, by an experience that recalls that of John Wesley at Aldersgate Street in 1736, he could say : " I felt some presence with me, and knew that Jesus had heard me and had come to seek me." His further experiences, his military service, his flight into Ankole, his first essays in preaching, his prayers, his renunciations, his resolute celibacy, his ultimate baptism and Confirmation at the age of 30, his sense of missionary vocation, are told at length by Albert Lloyd. For my present purpose it is enough to say that to Toro he came shortly before the advent of Bishop Tucker ; and that, once in Toro, the giant range of Ruwenzori, far from proving a barrier, became a fresh missionary challenge of the most imperious kind. To him it was not *what* was beyond, but *who* were beyond. He entreated the king. He made the arduous ascent. " I saw," he said, " the great country stretching out into the distance before me. A voice with me seemed to say : ' Over there in that country are thousands in heathen darkness. No one has ever been there to tell them about Jesus.' I knew at that moment that God was calling me."

Of Apolo's sufferings on that other side, how twice over he was nearly slain by the chief of Mboga, how twice over he returned to his God-given task, Lloyd told me as we journeyed to visit him in those far-off wilds. The journey to Mboga is unique. Down escarpment after escarpment we descended from the heights of Toro. First there is a broad, park-like terrace that the wild beasts have made peculiarly their own. Here we found fresh footprints of the elephant, buffalo, leopard, hyena, ant-bear, and buck. At night a lion was roaring close to our tent. A herd of buffaloes, most dangerous of all, approached close to our camp-fire at dusk. It felt like going to sleep in the Zoo with all the railings unbarred. After this animating zone we descended again sharply to the sultry plain of the Semliki, the powerful river that now divides the British from the Belgian sphere. Upon this plain abound water-buck and Uganda cob. Then, the passage of the Semliki being

Expansion Westward

achieved in man's primitive ferry, the dugout canoe, a further tramp in broiling heat brought us in two days to the grass-clad Alps of the Congo Belge, and here it was that in an experience of an unforgettable kind I met the man Apolo and his flock.

Picture to yourself first this uninhabited world of remoteness and wildness, this haunt of the wild beast, behind the Mountains of the Moon, at the very back of the beyond. Then conceive what it meant that out of the opposing mystery of hill and forest there should come to meet you, not pagans and savages, but a white-clad company of the Church of God. Here they were, their venerable pastor at their head, their chief at his side. Wonderful it was with them to climb to the plateau of their habitations, to see the Church they had built with their own hands to the glory of God, and the avenue of eucalyptus trees, leading from the running brook in which their first converts were baptized by the Rev. J. Callis. Right up to the church door we came, and dripping, and well-nigh dropping, we entered with them for a glad thanksgiving to God.

The Confirmation took place next day in the midst of the Holy Communion, after the

Nicene Creed. All was very simple, very orderly. Though for all these years this African clergyman had laboured alone in these wilds, nothing that he knew of church order had been overlooked. He had trained and prepared his candidates well. Each, according to the Uganda rule, had first been questioned in the Gospels of St. Matthew and St. John. Each had been approved by name by his Church Council. On the mud step of the sanctuary a leopard-skin was placed beneath the Bishop's chair. The candidates, all in white, knelt two by two upon a buckskin. There was a wonderful spirit in the church throughout the Confirmation, and at the Communion that followed. The old chief, who in earlier years had been Apolo's persecutor, and is now by God's grace his strenuous supporter, was the first to whom I administered the Sacrament. I could not but feel the miracle of it all. The building up of such a Church in such a land was so great an evidence of the wonder-working power of the Holy Spirit. There was nothing new or bizarre about it. One was sharing there in the one Holy Catholic and Apostolic fellowship.

Nor was evidence lacking that this same sense of incorporation into a divine fellowship was the joy of these people also. I shall not forget the testimony of one of their leaders. It was on the Monday, at a meeting in their school, that this man rose up and, speaking of their moral peril during Apolo's absence, said : " We were as wild beasts returning into the jungle, but are now gathered back again into the flock of Christ." The flock of Christ, where he desired to be— his *home*. What words to reach the ears upon the borders of the Congo Forest ! The African, far from being pressed, is himself pressing into " the Kingdom." Education in the Christian Gospel he will have. For in the flock of Christ he finds himself no alien, but at home : " Lo there was he born." Long ago, in beautiful and striking imagery, the Psalmist had depicted Sion as the metropolis of the universal Kingdom of God, and anticipated the day when all nations would be adopted into it as its citizens. Of Sion it would be reported that even the far-off " Morian," the African, " was born in her " and would own her as his spiritual home. Now in my own ears that prophecy was being fulfilled. More than that, of this Mboga Church, so loyal, so active, flung out far beyond the sphere even of any organized missionary activity, one felt in quite a peculiar degree that the Builder and Maker was God. Here was faith for once translated into sight. Here was the Holy Spirit at work, extending the confines of the Church beyond our farthest expectations, beyond our own limited or laggard essays, making its expansion His own.

The Mboga mission leaves upon the mind certain abiding impressions. You see here as in some special test case the convincing effects of native evangelization. " As a missionary," writes the Bishop of Uganda, " Apolo Kivebulaya is outstanding in the Uganda Church; but he is certainly not unique. It is perhaps hardly realized at home how much and how often the missionary extension of the Uganda Church has been the work of native evangelists. They have faced savage conditions of life, a strange language, shortage of food, exile, and persecution in the cause of Christ, and they have won through."

But their very readiness to go forth as missionaries only throws upon the Church the greater responsibility of leadership and of training. " They are apt to be," as the Bishop candidly warns us, " independent and autocratic, for they are essentially

Expansion Westward

a ruling race. Their enthusiasm is sometimes short-lived." For long years to come it will be the duty of the mother Church not only to educate a native ministry in whatever may be possible in the way of spiritual and administrative knowledge, but far more to support them in the way of personal self-discipline and in habits of devotion. In a later chapter we shall refer more fully to this urgent problem. For the moment we may well pause to offer up a prayer of sincere thanksgiving to God, that by His uplifting power to so great an extent in the last generation the extension of His Church in Middle Africa has made such amazing advances, and that the spiritual bridge across Africa of which Krapf dreamed is so near accomplishment.

MAP OF BUSOGA AND THE EASTERN PROVINCE

CHAPTER V

BUSOGA

IN the east of Uganda, between the districts of Buganda and Elgon, almost converted into an island by its belt of lakes and rivers, and for the most part hidden in swamp or forest, lies Busoga. To think of Busoga is to think of a land whose people have seemed weary, not with age but with discouragement; whose climate spells the very name of lethargy; and whose history has seemed to be too often a terrorized existence. Bishop Tucker wrote in 1899 :—

> The climate of Busoga is not an invigorating one. All nature seems to be suffering from limpness and lack of energy. What wonder if the human frame should yield to such an enervating condition? But, even more than the body, it is the mind that suffers. The powers of darkness were entrenched as in an impregnable stronghold, and it was evident that only by the might of the " stronger than the strong man armed " could they be dispossessed of that sovereignty over the mind and consciences of the Basoga which for so long ages they had exercised.

A bitter and abiding heritage indeed; and perhaps nowhere else in Uganda is this psychic pressure of evil to be felt in anything like the same degree. You have only to sit alone on the veranda in the short African twilight, when the mind is receptive to impressions, to feel this ominous, unaccountable shadow that preys upon life. It is not difficult then to imagine how in the beautiful, evergreen forests, below the rank mass of undergrowth, something real and sinister is urging those cruel, tightly-clinging creepers to choke slowly and surely the life out of the trees to which they cling; that in this chill, penetrating miasma rising from the swamps is something heavy and malevolent, ready to weave into the minds and souls of the people its web of abominable emotions.

A strange, dark land, Busoga, where even to-day a missionary can write : " The matron of our boarding school, who is one of the finest African women I know, came to me the other day and said that one of the new teachers was a witch. I was inclined to take it almost as a joke, but she and the children were terrified, and I have had to send the girl away." Again, " a small boy was brought to the hospital. He had been found on the road in a fit. He sits hunched up on the veranda like a frightened bird with a broken wing. He was unspeakably dirty, but none of the other men, who all happened to be peasants, would go near him to wash or help him in any way. They were terrified, and said he was possessed by an evil spirit."

And alongside this story of fear and hidden happenings runs the tale of a sequence of almost incomparable tragedies. From time immemorial this naturally rich and fertile land has been the happy hunting-ground of its formidable neighbours, the Baganda, who enslaved thousands of its men and women. They also forced them to pay a yearly tax of ivory, cattle, barkcloth, hoes, and native produce. This engendered a bitterness which is apparent, among the older peasants at least, to this day. The population of southern Busoga has been practically wiped out by sleeping sickness. Two disastrous famines—the one in 1900, and the other in 1908—carried off thousands of the people. Plague has been an ever-increasing trouble, and is only now being properly treated. In its long history it has probably accounted for more fear and death than famine ever did. There was nothing to make for progress in all this most unhappy land. There was no king, no unifying force. The country was divided among the chiefs, each exceedingly distrustful of the others, and in a constant state of warfare over small local rights. What wonder that to the arrogant and conquering Baganda this languid, crushed people seemed " scarcely worthy of the name of men " !

Yet this despised, unattractive little country made history for Buganda. Here Bishop Hannington in 1885, creeping in by a back way as the nervous natives thought, fell a prey to their suspicions, and was murdered. Here Pilkington, serving as an interpreter on the side of the natives against the Sudanese in the Nubian rebellion of 1897, fell dead on the plains of Bukaleba. Here, too, at the same time Norman Macdonald, Major Thruston, Drs. Wilson and Scott met their deaths. These stories, blazoned through every town in England and Scotland, gave a fresh impetus to the interest in the Church's story of its struggles in Uganda, and indeed in the whole of Africa.

Missionary work began in Busoga in 1891, when Mr. F. C. Smith was sent there from Buganda. In 1892 Mr. Roscoe, too, opened up work, but almost immediately he and Smith had to withdraw. In 1894 Crabtree and Rowling came from Kavirondo, and

Busoga

the latter stayed three years and did great work with his printing-press, turning out St. Matthew's Gospel and other books in Lusoga, and incidentally giving a start to the first Baganda boys who ever learnt to print. It is not difficult to imagine that in this atmosphere of suspicion and ignorance the work made but slow progress. In 1900 there were only two baptisms recorded in the whole of Busoga.

But gradually conditions became more heartening. The coming of the Rev. S. R. Skeens to Iganga in 1899 was a true Godsend to the Basoga, and his name is still a household word. He was able to record a thousand baptisms in 1911, and in 1912 that the Basoga had contributed Rs 4000 to their own church support. Better witness even than this to faithful work is a paragraph in a letter from him in 1913, in which he says : " Quite recently we were able to send fifteen young Basoga Christians as missionaries to Ng'ora. . . . From the whole of the Basoga Christians fifty of these young missionaries have been sent out now to heathen countries." As to the reality of the enthusiasm of these home-loving people bred in stubborn and unprogressive Busoga, let one of themselves speak. He was home on furlough at Iganga, and he held, with others, a meeting to tell what they had done on their first term of service. " You remember," he says at the end of his speech, " how the Baganda came to us and preached the Gospel ? Then they jumped over us and went to Bukedi. Let us Basoga do the same : let us first go to the Teso people, and afterwards to Karamoja."

The tide was slowly coming in, but as the flow was remarkable, so too was the ebb. The two went together inevitably. The retarding forces were so dominant. It is like watching some titanic mammoth playing with helpless and tormented souls. Drink and immorality—in the old pagan days firmly and often brutally condemned on purely utilitarian grounds—with the passing of paganism gained firm foothold. Christian opposition became ineffective. To the onlooker the actual achievement of Christianity was barely visible among the victims of these devastating temptations.

It is the more remarkable that under conditions so exacting the Church in the years that have followed has made that headway which is now apparent in many directions. I have many happy memories of Busoga. For a time it was my home.

I like to think of a first Confirmation at Kamuli ; of a Holy Week spent at Kaliro ; of journeys in the company of that veteran hero, the Rev. Allen Wilson, who, stationed here in 1896, true shepherd that he is, had never, except for occasional furloughs, left the district. Great days I have had with H. A. Brewer, head of our school work in Busoga, who, with his keen, infectious spirit has brought home to Europeans and natives alike the true life of Christianity.

For travellers in Busoga, Iganga is a central place of call. Iganga is a station of straight little red roads and mighty mvule trees, whose roots seem eternally to stand in pools of fierce, merciless sunshine. It was in 1901 that the first European women arrived there, and their coming was followed by a veritable season of terror. Night after night the fire-alarm had to be sounded, and the station was almost burnt to the ground by the suspicious natives. But, though they lost almost everything that they had, those intrepid women, Miss Pilgrim and Miss Brewer, were not to be frightened away ; and gradually the attack ceased. It was Iganga that fought the famine of 1908, and it was near Iganga that the first " sleeping camp " was formed.

It was certainly the mission's unfailing help to the distressed and panic-stricken people in these times of famine and sickness that somewhat allayed their fear of the foreigner. There is an old native woman who often tells how the white woman doctor saved Iganga district in a particularly bad outbreak of plague, how, single-handed, she fought the fatalism and indifference of the people, how every evening, when the heavy day's work was done, she bicycled mile after mile to burn infected huts. This was Miss Amy Welsh, who has worked there for twenty years. There is now a flourishing girls' boarding school in Iganga, which was founded by Miss Welsh as a home for plague and famine orphans in 1909. It has had many vicissitudes since then, but the coming of Miss Florence Allshorn in 1920 brought a change which can be seen in its present high standard of efficiency.

So here, too, in Busoga this play of vital liberating forces is being enacted. Here, too, Christian education has made, and is making, a new people of the middle and upper strata of the Basoga. Look at these eager boys on the Kamuli or Iganga or Kaliro football fields. Watch them bending over their books and slates long after school-hours are over, ambitious to secure a scholarship for Budo in Uganda. See them coming back from Budo to the school reunion, full of cheer and hope. More wonderful still, where woman has ranked a little lower than a cow for untold generations, listen to the girls shyly but persistently demanding to be taught as the boys, and one here refusing to be sold when the time for marriage comes. Go into a women's committee and, if you have patience to sit for several hours, listen with what wisdom they thrash out the difficulties of a moral problem, or, confronted with a batch of newly trained teachers to be sent out to the surrounding districts, with what care they settle where each girl shall be placed. Read this description of a gathering of the Mothers' Union at Kamuli : " On Wednesday afternoon motors began to roll up with chiefs' wives beautifully dressed. The secretary from Kaliro, a very enterprising native woman, had on her own initiative hired a motor-van, and the women each paid their share. One woman had had a three hours' walk in the grilling sun. We dispensed tea to 214 members, and afterwards had an animated committee meeting."

What a story of fitful sunshine and heavy shadows it is ! But the sunshine is gaining ground. Because of it Busoga is no longer a land separate and apart, only praying to be left alone. She is entering upon a new and alert youth. She is becoming conscious that in the industrial world her own produce need not be behind, that she has excellent and almost unlimited timber, that she is prolific in skins, that she has a wealth of jutes and fibres, that there is more to be done than to sit idly in the sun and see cotton grow and food ripen. She watches while the great English Government chooses her land through which to engineer railways, and gains a new vision of the value of that land. She has an incredible and baffling patience, but out of it may still be born a power of constructive purpose that will turn into inestimable virtue those characteristics that have kept her behind so long. Perhaps more than all this group of peoples she knows her need of a leader, and we have the greatest of all Leaders to give her.

CHAPTER VI

MOUNT ELGON AND THE MASS MOVEMENT

THE Protectorate of Uganda has a geographical compactness of its own. For most purposes of approach the Great Lake has been the natural avenue. It forms a boundary to the south and south-east which is at all events well defined. The River Nile, running for the first 500 miles of its great course through Uganda, bisects the present Protectorate into two roughly equal parts, while east and west, as though still further to accentuate its boundary lines, the mountain masses of Elgon and Ruwenzori stand up as sentinels against all comers. Of Ruwenzori and the Toro mission at its base we have already written.

We have now to tell of a yet greater expansion which has taken place to the east in the last twenty-five years, and which has made of Mount Elgon a similar strategic point. If the jubilee must commemorate in profound thanksgiving to God the initial conflict and self-sacrifice in the older missions to the west, it will be with an enthusiasm not one whit less that it will acknowledge the amazing advances to the east. For in no part of the world in recent years can the Church record more remarkable happenings than those of the mass movements of the Elgon district, the social transformation of Teso, or the opening up of the Nilotic regions of Lango, Gulu, and Kitgum toward the Sudan.

It was in November, 1900, that the Rev. W. A. Crabtree, who had been engaged in linguistic work at Gayaza, started with his wife for a holiday, proposing to travel into what was then the unexplored region often called Bukedi. To Mount Elgon he came, and to Nabumale upon the slope of Nkoko Njeru, a fine buttress of Elgon on its southwest side. So attractive did he find the prospect, so great the opportunities among the Bagishu people, that, with the Bishop's consent, he never returned from that holiday tour; and from that day to this, with the exception of a brief interval, the station of Nabumale has been the envy of all comers, and the centre of an ever-growing religious and social activity.

Elgon is at the present time pre-eminently the land of the mass movement. The mass movement may here be studied in all its

Mount Elgon and Mass Movement 99

many-sided problems, and I shall never forget my first experience of it. Of late years a motor road takes you direct from Jinja on the Great Lake to Mbale, the administrative centre of the Elgon district, by way of Busiya. Mbale will, in fact, shortly be reached by the Uganda Railway. Up to 1920 the conventional route was still that followed by Crabtree in 1900, and so well described by Purvis in 1903, across the Mpologoma River at the Terinyi Ferry. My travelling-companion was Canon E. S. Daniell, head of the Mukono College, and as we were slowly punted down a long avenue of papyrus in blazing noon in the hollowed-out trunk of a tree, the side-car of the motor-cycle protruding gauntly over the edge of this primitive vessel, one could not but cogitate both upon the incongruities of contemporary travel, and upon the calm enjoyments still accessible to the traveller in a primitive land. Once in sight, however, of the opposite shore reflections were of another kind. For the nature of our reception soon became apparent. The whole Christian community of the place turned out to welcome us. They were drawn up in a long line flanking either side of the road, clapping and cheering with much spirit as we stepped ashore. We had a short service with them. Here to the east among these wild tribes was that same note of welcome as in the remote fastnesses of Mboga to the west. It was indeed affecting to find that we who had come to give were rather recipients than bestowers of Christian brotherhood. At the very outset of our visit we were in the embrace of that Christian fellowship of which these primitive people were now partakers as much as we.

But this Terinyi greeting was, as we were soon to find, but a meagre preface to what was to follow. Some forty miles still intervened between us and Nabumale, our headquarters ; and ten times over, at intervals of abour four miles, this amazing welcome took place. Now and again we might seem to be in the midst of a virgin African jungle. No sign would indicate population. Yet here was this white and dark avenue of living forms. No haphazard gatherings these. In each case the teacher was at their head. In each case we asked who had been baptized, who were reading—that is, preparing as catechumens for baptism—and who were coming next day to be confirmed at Mbale. At Mbale itself the crowd was so great that we bade them accompany us to their

Mount Elgon and Mass Movement 101

big, newly-built church. Here even only a section could find entrance, and the rest sat on the ground outside, the unglazed windows of the church enabling them to take an unhindered part. At Nabumale, ten miles beyond, high on the slopes of Mount Elgon, the welcome was half a mile in length. I have never seen anything like it, and as we passed each figure rose up and raced after us. About 2000, mostly heathen, were crammed into Nabumale church, and a large number clustered outside.

How has all this come about? Twenty years before, as narrated above, Mr. and Mrs. Crabtree had come to this hill country on a holiday adventure, and had had permission to stay. After three years they were succeeded by the Rev. and Mrs. J. B. Purvis, of whose early struggles with the Bagishu problems—language, witchcraft, morals, and education—you may read in Purvis's graphic story. Steadily Purvis was at work, translating, teaching, organizing. Teachers were sent out northward, westward, southward, to Palisa, Mbale, Bukedeya, Kumi, and even Ng'ora.

A year later (1904) the first church was opened by Bishop Tucker, accompanied by Archdeacon Walker and the Rev. T. R.

(afterwards Archdeacon) Buckley. Then in 1905 came Miss Pilgrim, " a qualified nurse, sensible woman, and true missionary," and by her wisdom and kindly skill the foundations of women's work in that wild region were laid. Walter Holden followed—the translator of the Gospels into the local speech. Later, one by one, came Agnes Morris, H. B. Ladbury, J. E. M. Hannington (the Bishop's son), H. K. Banks, H. Mathers, and A. J. Leech; and, more recently still, Miss A. E. Allen and Miss Dorothy Smith.

One by one they have held the fort upon the mountain-side at Nabumale, or at Mbale on the plain—until in most cases health failed. When I first reached Nabumale the Rev. H. K. Banks and his wife (*née* Agnes Morris) were quite alone. I found Banks running single-handed (1) a church and all that it involves, (2) a day school, (3) a teachers' centre, (4) a carpenters' training-shop, (5) his principal effort, a boys' boarding school, in which some of the chiefs were learning farming, carpentering, etc., (6) plantations spread over 200 acres, bearing crops of coffee, cotton, millet, beans, upon which his school was fed and trained. Self-taught, he had erected his own buildings.

Mount Elgon and Mass Movement 103

Nay—such is the comity of missions, (as he loves to record) he had taught three Roman priests who superintended the R.C. mission hard by how to build *their* church, sitting aloft astride the roof-beam and giving them instructions as they toiled below!

One Englishman and his wife for all this vast, wild land of the mass movement and of the mountain peoples! Could this frail succession of missionaries upon yonder hillside, never more than one or two at a time, account for all my eyes had seen of ordered congregations and ardent welcome as I came along? How, then, has the Church in this short space of seventeen years become established in such a way that throughout this large district, through Bugwere, Budama, Bugishu, even among the mountain ridges and dales of Mount Elgon, Christian communities are everywhere to be found? How have they become organically connected with each other, and with their centre, ready for baptism, Confirmation, the Holy Communion itself, and honouring profoundly the constitution of the Church? How has this mass movement been met and disciplined and organized, so far as it has been, for Christ and His Kingdom? For, admitting all the imperfections of the body, you have still the marvel of its structure—its organization—rising up and facing you in the most astounding way, in plain and jungle, forest and hill. To account for this ever-arresting phenomenon you must rightly estimate the *missionary zeal of the Uganda native clergy*, the African *teacher-instinct*, and, behind all, the imperious *urge of the mass movement spirit*.

Who is this who seems to be everywhere at once in this Nabumale area, this ubiquitous man, sometimes on a bicycle, sometimes on foot, but always *there*? I have told you of Apolo Kivebulaya, missionary of Mboga and the Congo Forest. I must now introduce to you another brother clergyman, less known to fame, but none the less meriting it, Kezekiya Bekabye. With flashing eye and a glorious smile, Kezekiya is a true pastor. Organizer, financier, but supremely the pastor, he has been my companion over hill and dale. I have visited scores of his little congregations on mountain and plain. Everything is in order. His people meet you at the trysting-place. His chiefs are awaiting you. His confirmation candidates are all there. He knows them and they know him and love him. Is he one of themselves? Is this his native land? Does he like being there? Far from it.

Mount Elgon and Mass Movement

He is a missionary from Buganda, living alone, for his wife has had to remain behind. Yet here he is, a veritable pillar in the house of his God. In Busiya, nearer the lake, is the Rev. Saulo Namuyenga, tall, dignified, reserved, another Muganda missionary. Only these two clergymen there were when I first went to Elgon; but in their charge were the whole corps of teachers, on whom all the separate flocks depend.

The African teacher-instinct is a constant surprise. In England this desire to be a teacher is rare. An Englishman will do almost any kind of work for the Church rather than teach. In Africa it is the reverse. Go where you will among the Bantu tribes, it is apparently a common aspiration to come forward as the teacher of your village. Naturally these teachers are often crude and ill-informed. In most cases their sole qualification, and slight enough it is, is Confirmation. They are meagrely paid. Yet they are eager to learn. And they are ambitious to secure admission to those classes which enable them grade by grade to ascend, until they get the coveted " Third Letter " or even enter the diaconate. A further characteristic : they seem as Africans instinctively to appreciate organization.

In middle Africa you find territorial divisions and sub-divisions analogous to our own. You find counties, districts, townships, parishes. A native clergyman has not only a large district of his own, but within this he has perhaps ten *mirukas*, each with six, eight, or ten village congregations, each with its own teacher. Thus he has perhaps eighty or a hundred teachers whom he can convene for conference, with or without their flocks, by the rapid African convention of a circular letter. By this system, imported into the outlying districts from Buganda, the mass movement area, which would be totally beyond the management of one European, can be directed. It is the just pride of the Uganda Mission that through all its length it is self-supporting, self-governing, self-expanding. The rapid expansion of the work is due largely to the native genius for organization, and to the real devotion of native clergy and teachers.

All this, however, in a world of its own like Elgon would be quite in vain without that one thing more, most remarkable of all. It is that upward " urge," as it has been called, working in the very souls of the people themselves. It is the deep-seated aspiration, born of contact with civilized man, to be quit of their backwardness and their nakedness, and to secure some incorporation, however remote, in the embrace of that family of privilege in which they instinctively feel they have a rightful inheritance. It would be unfair to designate this movement as essentially religious. As you pass down those long lines of dark, naked figures, that greet you so expectantly on the road every few miles, it is to feel often, as you look into their eyes, the pathos of a " backwardness " so backward as to give you the strange feeling that you are with " sub-men " rather than with *men*. Theirs is a hunger, not I think for a spiritual, as much as for a human affinity. They crave almost like wounded animals for human compassion. Stripped even of the little they possess by the robbers—disease, cruelty, and neglect, they wait by the roadside of life looking for some Samaritan to get down and bind up their wounds, pouring in the oil of ordinary human kindness.

Yet as has been so well said with regard to the similar movement in India[1] : " There is no doubt that a mass movement is a movement of God's Holy Spirit on men. Over the face of the waters that are often

[1] C.M.S. Delegation to India, 1921-2, Report, p. 69.

very dark the Spirit of God is moving to prepare the way for the commanding Word that shall bring light. Through different agencies He breaks down the prejudice and conservatism of generations. He moves people to come. The Church must receive those that respond. It is God's open door : we must enter in. It is God's hand beckoning us to cast the net where the shoals of fish are to be discerned. It is God's call to reap the fields white unto harvest." It is when viewed in this temper of mind that much that might seem bizarre or disappointing is understood. The acceptance of the Christian religion by communities may lack the depth of its acceptance by individual souls. Elgon has never, like Uganda, had its hour of persecution. Shepherds have been far too few to lead the flock one by one. Morally this community-movement makes slow advance. Polygamy dies hard. The ghastly heritage of vice overwhelms these weak-willed peoples. The African, to quote Sir Harry Johnston again, is quick to accept, quick to lose Christianity. It will take generations, it may be, to alter moral codes among these multitudes whose passions are so strong, and whose means of grace are so few. Make, however, what reservations,

Mount Elgon and Mass Movement

what strictures we will, can we question the desire of the Chief Shepherd for these sheep of His in this far wilderness? Can we question for a moment the duty of His Church? Surely, if ever sheer pity could touch the heart, it is here amid these child-tribes of Mount Elgon. If any song of praise goes up to our great Redeemer through this Uganda jubilee it must be that the venture of faith that began at Mengo has in so short a space of time reached out the hand of compassion to these peoples of the Eastern Province and has already gathered such numbers of them into His flock.

This mass movement district around Mount Elgon forms the southern portion of the new diocese of the Upper Nile,[1] and thus comes at this critical stage in its history under the care of Bishop Kitching, who was one of the pioneers at Mbale.

Three scenes from this mass movement area remain indelibly impressed upon my mind. For either pathos or joy they are hard to rival. Picture to yourself a veritable wall of a mountain pass towering above you, and such a sweltering noon as only mid-Africa can give. Prostrate

[1] The diocese of the Upper Nile comprises the northern and north-eastern districts of the Uganda Protectorate and two provinces (Mongalla and Bahr el Ghazal) of the Southern Sudan.

and parched, you are literally hauled up what you believed to be the final ascent, only to find the skyline ever higher above your head. As you near the summit something of a strange ornamentation seems to catch your eye, like the balls upon the coronet of an earl. It cannot be—yet it actually *is*— a row of heads ! It is a whole congregation waiting for you, expectant for you, just as you are—all dripping and broken, with no ghost of a breath left in you—to *preach* ! It was a wonderful sight when the grassy plateau ultimately was gained. Here were two congregations sitting upon the ground. Hot tea can do much at any time. And, after this light refreshment, it was a stirring thing to address that eager company upon the ridge, valley-deeps opening sheer on either side, and the summit of Elgon veiled still in mists. Memorable also was the joyous abandon with which these mountain folk flung themselves down in a living cascade upon the other slope of the pass, their young boys and girls alighting with perfect poise and ease upon projecting rocks, to gather up again in the valley below in a densely crowded church. Where else could mountaineer find such an ovation or preacher such a setting for a sermon !

Mount Elgon and Mass Movement 111

Imagine next upon a lower foothill of Mount Elgon another company, yet larger. Round a roughly built church some 4000 people are congregated. Each had picked two large banana-leaves, one for a groundsheet, the other for a sunshade ! Nearly all were heathen. Yet there were Christians, too, packed inside the church. About a hundred had been confirmed. They must be considered first. There was, of course, only one service for such an occasion. We had agreed on it beforehand. So Kezekiya and I robed in the government rest-house, and, with the thirty-four teachers of the district in their white kansus two and two before us, we proceeded slowly into and through the large company, and round the church, singing " *Katonda twagala*," the Luganda version of " Yes, Jesus loves me," to the familiar tune. All these people seemed to know it or to catch it. They stood and just roared it forth. Then during the long collection we again went outside and did what we could, by word and hymn and prayer among the interminable rows of heathen people. Inside followed the crowning moment. Ninety communicated. Afterwards there was, as invariably, a conference of teachers, to ascertain their needs: books it might be, or provision for training, or a football! Here one matter weighed particularly upon them. They wanted a European to teach them. They will do the preaching, far better than we can. Their one demand was for some white man to tell them what it is they are to preach. I wish that any who protest that we are pressing our religion upon these peoples against their will could have felt, as I did, the insistence of these thirty-four young Africans! Here, at all events, the pressure is all the other way.

Is this religious expression of these backward peoples superficial? Is this merely an evanescent collective emotion—an excitement for the moment only? Come to yet one more of Elgon's spurs. Below you sweeps northward the plain of Teso, far into the misty haze of the Sudan. It is evening, and up the glens and defiles of the mountainside are creeping small companies to a little church upon the higher level. For to-morrow is the Confirmation, and now at 5.30 p.m., before the sun sets at six o'clock, there is to be a preparation service. Darker and darker grow the poles of the church against the flaming orange of the sunset; and in the gathering twilight a voice at the back of the church is heard upraised in prayer, gentle, entreating, almost heartbroken. This is the burden of it : " Lord, Thou knowest that we have fallen away from Thy laws. Not one of us is living according to Thy Will." Are these submen ? Are they not, with all their backwardness, made in the image of God ! Of all things divine in man, is not Carlyle right that this is most divine—*repentance* ? Shall not He Who despises not the sighing of the contrite heart find here that which He seeks ?

A wonderful thing is this mass movement. Quite clearly the only men who can guide and discipline and inspire it are these humble and lowly teachers and, as we have seen, they are often ignorant and ill-equipped for their responsible work. The training of the teachers, here in Africa as in India, must be for long years to come the primary concern of the Church.

MAP SHOWING CLOSE RELATION OF UGANDA TO THE SUDAN

The through communication between Khartoum and Kampala is shown by (*a*) the broad black line of the navigable Nile from Khartoum to Mongalla, (*b*) the motor road from Mongalla to Tororo, (*c*) rail thence to Nairobi, and (*d*) road to Kampalla. The railway, Tororo to Jinja, is now under construction.

CHAPTER VII

TESO AND THE NEW MODEL

THE various districts that compose the Uganda Protectorate are distinguished in turn by a certain variety. If at the centre the somewhat monotonous alternation of swamp and hill has a kind of " ridge-and-furrow " sameness of its own, the districts upon the circumference possess more happily marked characteristics. Toro in its cache among the hills, Elgon with its sweeping curves of mountain and plain, Entebbe with its Riviera setting, Masindi with its park-like approaches, must leave each its distinctive impress upon the memory. Of none is this more observable than of Teso. With Teso, sloping northward toward Abyssinia, you enter upon conditions that at once arrest you as unlike any you have yet seen in the Protectorate. You seem to be in a new kind of Africa—flat, fertile, and largely treeless. Similarly when you reach Ng'ora, at the centre of Teso, you find a new missionary regime. If we take stock of the various missionary experiments that have sprung up within the one Uganda Mission there is none that should more quickly evoke our attention than this in Teso. Alike in its industrial, its educational, and its moral aspects, it has ideas to contribute to the future training of the African that are of an important kind.

Although it would be meaningless flattery to say of any part of Equatorial Africa that all nature is smiling and gay, one ought in fairness to concede to Teso that herein nature is less aggressively obstinate or truculent or moody than in general. Teso, as I have said, is comparatively open country. Bishop Kitching felicitously named his volume upon Teso "The Backwaters of the Nile." The river, broadening out into this huge "backwater," called in its various ramifications Lake Kioga, Lake Salisbury, Lake Gedge, not only penetrates at many an unsuspected turning into the low-lying Teso, but offers to its rich soil the nutriment of its waters, and to its produce of cotton a navigable waterway. When the Rev. J. B. Purvis first entered Teso (and I think he was the pioneer) it was by Lake Kioga that he came. These waters are, if sometimes the despair of the traveller, stranding him for hours or days, at other times his delight.

Teso and the New Model 117

Where else is there such duck-shooting ? Where else such warmth and colour and sport combined ? To sit, gun on knee, under the blazing sun in the bows of a hollowed-out log, punted noiselessly through a lush carpet of richest vegetation, till the faint squirrel-coloured streak upon the lake surface warns you that your whistling-teal are near, and all is intense and alert—is something for which to give thanks. Where else has the garden of the world such an expanse of water-lilies ! Purple and mauve, they seem to make amethyst the whole lake, while the cupolas of the white clouds towering to infinite heights in the deep blue of the sky marble by their reflection this bright surface. I like to think of a Sunday morning service upon a deck only a few inches above the water with natives and crew, and a Scots skipper to read the lesson, as we gently steamed mile after mile through these purple water-lilies. Into this flat, fertile, well-watered country, unknown to civilized man but twenty-five years ago, you now come by motor northward from Elgon to find good roads, with cotton fields extending as far as the eye can reach on either side. An ordered agricultural world. Who are its people ? By what processes have these changes been so speedily brought into effect?

According to the Uganda census of 1921 the people of Teso form by far the largest tribe in the Protectorate after the Baganda themselves. They are a Nilotic people, and speak an impossible click-clack Nilotic speech. By Nilotic we mean those tribes upon the middle waters of the Nile, such as the Acholi, the Dinka, the Shilluk, the Lango, the Teso, the Karamojans, that dwell northward of the Bantu negroids and have linguistic and tribal peculiarities all their own. Less of a chocolate-brown, more of a grey-black than the Baganda, these Teso people are tall and spindle-legged in build, and warm-hearted and cheerful by temperament. A merciful Providence has ordained that in their barbarous speech the one word " *yoga* " means " Good morning," " Good night," " How are you ? " " Thank you," " Well done ! " To hear the stentorian *yoga* in response is invigorating.

Among Europeans the protevangelist of the Teso people is the Rt. Rev. A. L. Kitching, now their bishop. Coming to Teso in 1908, with Archdeacon Buckley's help and advice, he selected Ng'ora for the C.M.S. head-quarters. To his linguistic gifts

Teso and the New Model

is due the feat of reducing their dumbfoundering language first into coherent verbal equivalents, next into grammar, and then of handing to them the four Gospels and the Acts of the Apostles in their own tongue. The Bishop has himself told me of his early struggles : how for hour after hour, till the exact listening grew exhausting, he would collect the sounds a boy would make to denote objects around him ; and next of the infinitely more exhausting listening for the adjectives and verbs.

After six months Kitching was joined by H. G. Dillistone, the builder, and later by W. S. Syson the educationist. To this trio, probably the only three Englishmen who by 1920 had ever mastered the Teso language, is due the lay-out of the station (in itself one of the best planned in Uganda), but far more the planning of the mission's life and policy.

Dr. Garfield Williams in his " Report upon East African Education " emphasizes the necessity of educating the African primarily for his own African land and his own African life. All training-institutions, he says, must have manual training as an educational subject enthusiastically developed, and a teacher who is incompetent to give manual training, or who has not sufficient enthusiasm to do it, must be considered incompetent. It is this technical and agricultural side of education which has been specially developed in Teso. The Ng'ora high school is one of a chain of schools for chiefs' sons flung out along the north-eastern frontier of the Protectorate. Beginning with the Maseno School in Kavirondo, you find these schools at Nabumale, Ng'ora, Gulu, and even so far north as Juba in the Sudan; and what they have accomplished in stemming the southward influence of Islam it would be hard to measure. They follow certain clearly marked lines. Each is in charge of a European. Each is a boarding school. In each, so far as is possible, the Public School tradition of the devolution of responsibility is put into practice.

Trees, it has been observed, are scarce in Teso, but in Africa trees, if detrimental to agriculture, are nevertheless essential to architecture. Trees for building purposes you must have. Afforestation therefore is part of the curriculum; and it is a pleasant thing to see the school plantation of young tall nsambia trees, the future pillars of house, school, or church.

Teso and the New Model

Similarly ploughing is part of the school scheme. To the African the main agricultural implement is the hoe, but the hoe is tedious, and the rich fields of Teso await a more remunerative labour. So Syson introduced the plough and taught his boys to use it, the little stumpy oxen forming excellent draught-animals.

Syson also introduced the loom into Teso. In the Sudan the loom must have been in use through Egyptian influence for long years, and it is surprising that in a region like that of the Uganda Protectorate, with its natural produce of cotton and its accessibility to Arab civilization, the loom was not earlier known. Cotton goods have been so easily obtainable from England or India or Japan that the supply of the finished article has anticipated any demand for the means of manufacture. But the loom, like the plough, is calculated to benefit the African in more ways than one. Very creditable is the weaving that has been done, and, with patience, this industry should spread considerably.

Brickmaking here, as at so many mission stations, is *de rigeur*; and happy the station that finds the right clay close at hand. From the day of Alexander Mackay the

Church has been foremost in the teaching of useful handicrafts. In few things is this more evident than in the building craft. To look upon the excellent brickwork of Namirembe Cathedral, or of the churches at Toro, Ng'ora, Mbale, Iganga, Masindi, Kamuli, and a number more, to say nothing of a host of secular buildings, is to realize something of what Uganda owes to-day to its missionary builders, and to appreciate some of the interminable difficulties they have had to overcome in order to leave behind them such enduring monuments of their skill.

That which, however, gives to Teso its present importance, that which has transformed its outward appearance and has to so large an extent already transformed the habits of its people, has been the coming of cotton. Cotton is the name given to the soft cellular hairs that encircle the seed of the gossypium, a plant growing into a small shrub about twenty-four to thirty inches in height. A member of the mallow family (malvaceæ), it is allied to the mallow and the hollyhock. It has the same five-petalled inflorescence, the same delicate tints of primrose and pink. The black, bean-like seed is sown in June in drills about a yard apart, and the plant grows with astonishing

Teso and the New Model

rapidity, flowering in October, when, from the colouring of the corolla and the general height of the little shrub, the wilderness indeed appears to blossom as the rose. About seventy days pass and at Christmas time the boll is distended and bursting with its treasure of white lint. The seeming rose-garden is now snow-flaked with its charge of cotton-wool, and before it droops to the soil and loses its spotless texture eager hands must garner this precious harvest. For this cotton of Teso, as of Uganda generally and Nigeria, Nyassaland, and not least the Sudan, is now an asset of imperial importance.

As it was the early missionaries in our own North Country, the Cistercians at Furness, Fountains, and Kirkstall, who laid the foundations of our woollen industry by their introduction of sheep, so again, by all accounts, it was the Church that introduced cotton into Uganda. By way of giving to the natives a useful work to do, Mr. Borup on the western side and Mr. Purvis beyond the Nile on Mount Elgon began in 1904 to distribute cotton-seed among the chiefs. Little could either sower foresee the harvest in store.

In 1925, only twenty-one years later,

more than 200,000 bales of cotton were exported from Uganda. More than £3,000,000 came back in sterling to the native producer. When we reflect that to fill with cotton-lint one single bale three and a half acres of scrub must be first cleared, then dug, then sown, and hoed, the total already attained is seen to speak volumes for native industry.

The cotton harvest is now part of the people's life. First the lint is gathered into baskets, then brought to the wayside store or ginnery. Here for every 100 lbs. weighed, on government-tested scales, a receipt is given or a sum of cash at the current rate. The cotton is then transported by oxcart or motor-lorry to the ginnery, where by machine gins, worked by Africans, under European or Indian supervision, the black seed is eliminated from the lint, and the fluffy cotton pressed into bales of 450 lbs. From the ginnery the bales begin their long journey by road or rail or water until they reach their destination, Manchester or Bombay, at last.

In all this the Church has an eager share. Every school has its cotton patch. Every teacher thus has his small salary secured. Every little church has something in the

Teso and the New Model

way of maintenance to count upon, and throughout the whole land the glory of the garden is giving a new zest to honest work and a new purpose to life.

I have ventured to give to this Teso experiment the connotation of newness. I have tried to indicate how in its general lay-out—pastoral, agricultural, educational—there is the impression of something new in Teso. Is this also to be said in the region of character? In dealing with fruit we have to be on our guard against picked samples. The apples at the top of the hamper may well belie the general standard. In dealing with missionary produce the same caution is, of course, needful. The battle with past inheritance is so bitter. The disappointments are so keen, at least to those vanquished in the struggle. Still, making all deductions, there are memories in this matter of character which give one great hope among these Nilotic peoples.

On my first visit to Ng'ora I confirmed 292 candidates. The service was inevitably long. The words of confirmation were exceptionally difficult. Yet such was the reverence and dignity of the people who crammed every part of Ng'ora church that it might well have been an English congregation. I could not but note a pervading air of buoyancy, kindliness, and hope, and I was much struck with the collection : 550 rupees (£55) from these children of poverty and isolation, to whom each rupee (2*s.*) was as much as a £1 note to an English working man. Since then one still larger is reported, a thanksgiving collection in 1925 amounting to £250, much of it in cents (the hundredth part of a shilling), that took from 3 p.m. till 7 p.m. to count. The people are amazingly generous.

Another memory may be recalled. We met one morning the chiefs of the district at Kumi. They had something to say to us. They were a fine set of men, most of them young, picked out by the District Commissioner for their capacity of leadership. They surrounded us in two sides of a square, the front row sitting, the back row standing—a formal affair. Good boots they wore (English-made boots find their way in profusion to Teso !), and well-tailored dark blue serge coats. What had they to say ? Nothing about cows or taxes, as sometimes. One thing only. They must have Christian education for their womenfolk. They must have a woman educationist for their district. Christians most of them— old boys from Syson's school many of them —they have scarcely a chance of a Christian

Teso and the New Model

wife. Out of 425 I had just confirmed at Ng'ora and Bukedeya only twenty-two had been women. The figures spoke for themselves. I remember their determination to get that teacher and that teaching. It impressed me deeply. Happily soon after we were enabled to secure a noble pioneer in women's work for Teso in Miss May Gibbings. What a need it is! How hopeless is home-life unless it be supplied. One admired these young Africans for the way they insisted on it.

The seed, it is true, has been of the best, but the soil in Teso has been ready for it. It was my privilege in 1922 to dedicate the newly finished chapel at Ng'ora school. It had been paid for by a happy conceit. The donkeys of the King's African Rifles required maize. Syson undertook to grow the required supply; and out of this modest contract the materials for the chapel had been secured, and a beautiful little building it looked, as, crowded to the door, it awaited dedication. In the choir were seated the local government officials, just one of many tokens of their kindly attitude. To the right were forty old boys of the school, every one of them nursed in the school traditions, every one of them now a chief appointed by the British Administration, every one of them therefore in a post of authority somewhere in Teso.

Do such school traditions last ? It was my good fortune to visit the large remote area of Katakwi to the north of Lake Salisbury, falling away towards Karamojo and Abyssinia. This district was then under the chieftainship of Eriya Ochum, the first head boy of Ng'ora school. To be for a few days his guest, to meet his Christian wife, to be entertained at his own house, to see the roads he had engineered, the cotton he had planted, the church he had built, much more to see his demeanour towards his wife and his people, to worship with him, to talk with him, was to feel proud of this product of our school and deeply thankful that the ideals there engendered had borne such fruit. Others I could name. Through the school lies our way of advance. Though the moral antagonisms are tremendous, Christianity in Teso promises to mean not a name only, but a character and a life.

MAP OF THE NILE VALLEY, SHOWING THE FOUR DIOCESES

More particularly indicating the new diocese of the Upper Nile.

CHAPTER VIII

Lango: A Study in Animism

LANGO is the name given to the northernmost of the four districts which make up the Eastern Province of the Protectorate of Uganda. It lies beyond Lake Kioga. On the north it is bounded by Kitgum ; on the east by Teso. South and west, it is enclosed in the crook of the Nile, where between the two fresh-water seas, Lake Victoria and Lake Albert, the great river makes the first stage of its journey toward the Sudan. The people of Lango are like the Teso, of the type known as Nilotic. Both for character and capacity they stand out prominently. Their soil is rich, and largely suitable for cotton. Their country is well watered, and, as might be expected from the liberal supply of water and of cover, game is numerous and varied. Giraffe, rhinoceros, waterbuck, reedbuck, bushbuck, and Uganda cob, are frequently to be found. There are six large herds of elephant, and two of buffalo. The carnivorous animals—lion, leopard, serval, civet, and hyena—are numerous and destructive.

Of game birds there are duck, goose, teal, guinea-fowl, quail, snipe, and bustard. Mosquitos (largely of the anopheles genus) swarm almost everywhere.

It is of this interesting country, and of its people, that Mr. J. H. Driberg has written in his volume on " The Lango : A Nilotic Tribe of Uganda." This book, as the author himself declares, has been inspired by his affection for a race with whom he has lived and worked, as District Commissioner, for several years. " Brave, loyal, courteous, and hospitable, they have readily accorded me," he says, " a confidence greater than my deserving, and they will always remain more than a pleasant memory now that the exigencies of service have separated us." I have myself four times visited this country of Lango : twice from the north in 1921-2 with P. H. Lees, and twice in the same years with H. G. Dillistone, crossing over from Teso to Kalaki. Here are broad, hot, sunny roads, rising and falling monotonously from swamp to rise, from rise to swamp. Here are ever-increasing expanses of cotton on either side. " There is money in it," remarked a chief as we trudged along. And we must have passed " patches " of twenty or thirty acres in extent. Here are the long-limbed, lean, and muscular figures of the men, working on the soil, for in contrast with the practice of Bantu tribes, the men do all the hard work of cultivation. In Lango woman is respected. It is often urged against polygamy and the payment of dowries, that it results in the degradation of the woman to the position of being mere property. However true this may be elsewhere, it is very far from the truth among the Lango, whose womenfolk are treated with remarkable courtesy and consideration.

At intervals in the landscape rise the villages, which vary considerably in size from ten to 150 huts; not fenced in as by other Nilotic tribes by a thick euphorbia hedge or an earthen wall or a stockade of stout stakes, but—a testimony to the Lango independence of spirit—left open and unfortified against attack. Whether large or small the village is composed of married men's huts (*ot*), bachelor quarters (*otogo*), sheds (*goin*) for cooking and grinding, granaries, several kinds of chicken houses, and the cattle kraal. The ot is the property of the wife, and for each wife a man has to build a separate house and granaries, just as for each wife separate crops have to be cultivated. The otogo is a curious structure.

It resembles a dove-cot—so small it is—perched on stakes seven feet high, with a ladder to the tiny round aperture by which the boy squeezes to his bed at night. Moral reasons have been assigned for the erection of these weird structures. The most plausible reason is that they were to save the boys from being " magic-ed."

To visit Lango in the company of Mr. Driberg is, however, to secure very much more than a superficial glance at its people, their habits, and their dwellings. It is to be transported into that interior region so hard for the casual traveller to penetrate—the domain of their psychic relationships with the spirit-world, the region of their fears, their longings, their prayers.

Under the term " Jok," the Lango, like almost all Nilotics, conceive of the creative and prevailing spirit. The only description of Jok obtained is " like moving air." Jok, " like the wind or air is omnipresent, and like the wind, though the presence may be heard and appreciated, Jok has never been seen by any one. . . . His dwelling is everywhere : in trees, it may be, or in rocks and hills, in some springs and pools, especially in connexion with rain making, or more vaguely in the air."

Jok is the creative spirit. " To Jok is attributed the phenomenon of birth ; *jok ma tye iye omiyo dako nywal* (god that is within her causes a woman to bear)." It is Jok who created the two worlds of sky and earth in the Lango cosmology, together with their inhabitants. Jok, therefore, in his first appearance is a benevolent spirit, and benevolence is his natural tendency. From him come rich harvests. To him are due the seasons, with the rains, ensuring good crops, and the dry season for the joys of hunting. Jok, further, is a spirit that answers prayer. He is " always accessible to the prayers and inquiries of the faithful, and through the agency of his seers gives advice on all matters, great and small, but especially on such important problems as war and hunting."

Jok, nevertheless, is a jealous god and punishes neglect and scorn with severity. Disease, accidents, failure in hunting, losses of live-stock, and the many other tribulations of primitive man are punishments imposed by Jok for neglect or transgression. So powerful is Jok that proximity is dangerous, though such danger does not necessarily arise from Jok's ill will, but from the divine essence ; hence the avoidance of hills in which Jok may be immanent, and the evil consequences of building a village, even unwittingly, on the path which Jok is in the habit of traversing.

Three other terms in connexion with the religious conceptions of the Lango should be noted : *winyo, tipo,* and *ajoka.* The word *winyo,* usually meaning " bird," is applied to the guardian spirit which attends human beings and animals during life. *Tipo,* meaning " shade," is applied to the spirit or soul of human beings and certain animals. It is not clear what happens to the tipo at death, for it does not enter the grave with the corpse. It is, however, still associated with his personality, and is liable to be dangerous to the living, especially if the deceased met a violent death. Little shrines —built like diminutive huts about eighteen inches in diameter, supported on four posts a foot high—are set up for the tipo of ancestors as they are for Jok, to which small offerings of food are brought. From this shrine the tipo will give advice. It appears to be only the spirit of an immediate ancestor that occupies a shrine ; and the presumption is that ultimately the tipo is merged in Jok. The *ajoka,* or jok-man (a man of god), is the seer who ascertains and interprets Jok's will. Both men and women may be ajoka, but the most competent and renowned have been women. Witchcraft, Mr. Driberg assures us, is entirely abhorrent to the Lango, and the practisers of the art are severely dealt with. They are clubbed to death and their bodies are burnt. It is not surprising therefore that cases of witchcraft are rare.

Christianity, it is true, is only in its earliest stages in Lango. Yet on my first visit in 1921, when I conferred with the teachers at Kaduku, I found we had in that north-western portion thirty little " congregations," sixteen possessing some modest " church," and fourteen still " under trees." And when I visited Kalaki, our southern centre, it was to prove in the abundant church life there displayed how well and truly the foundations of Christianity had been laid by the brief service of W. G. S. Innes. Innes was only at Kalaki from November, 1909, to September, 1910, when he died of blackwater fever. Yet out of that short period of Christian leadership has arisen a remarkable situation. Remote from European aid, a faithful lay reader has shepherded the flock. A central school has been run. A good church has been built, wherein I saw fourteen couples united in Christian marriage, " with the ring," largely on the initiative of the women themselves. Scarcely could you have more convincing evidence of the readiness of these Lango brethren not only to receive but to perpetuate the Christian Faith. It is a comfort to record that after a long interval further European help has been available, and that the Rev. and Mrs. T. L. Lawrence are now at Lira.

Christianity is the natural sublimation of animism. Of these animist peoples it may fairly be declared that " the invisible things of Him from the creation of the world are clearly seen, being understood by the things that are made." To the animist Christianity seems all the time to be saying : " Whom ye ignorantly worship, Him declare I unto you." For this primitive worship, with its admitted limitations, is a real worship. As Mr. Driberg says : " It cannot be too often emphasized that religion is a much more important factor in the secular life of primitive peoples than it is with civilized communities—indeed, it is the most important factor of all." To whom therefore can the Christian Gospel of the Holy Spirit come with greater acceptability than to those who " by nature " apprehend the Deity as " moving air " ? Who, so much as those to whom

K

"a guardian spirit" is a matter of course, will welcome Christ's teaching on the ministry of angels? Where, more readily than among those who already entertain a " fear of God," will there be found that holy awe which in every age must be the beginning of heavenly wisdom? To what people, so much as to those who in their " ajoka" welcome the offices of the " man of God," is it our bounden duty to send such as may be true ministers of the Gospel?

Lango is a country full of hope. There are latent possibilities in the character of its people that are in some quarters little suspected. Lees and I were travelling one day from Lira to Kaduku, and at Lira some conversation had arisen about polygamy. Mr. Driberg has a good deal to say about polygamy. " The practice of polygamy," he says, " is intimately bound up with the social fabric of their existence." " Any attempt to enforce monogamy would be neither feasible nor desirable." At Lira similar language was used. " These fellows will never be satisfied with one wife; and you are simply butting against a brick wall in trying to make them so." On the road, as we halted for breakfast, another conversation took place. A woman, one of five wives of the local chief, asked this question :—

"Those two chiefs at——, were they confirmed on Sunday?"

"No. Why?"

"They are not good men. Both have other women."

"It's hard for a chief to keep to one wife, isn't it?"

"Not with the help of God. Look at Daudi."

"Daudi—has he no second wife, no other woman anywhere?"

"No, none."

To Daudi in due course we came, and to his wife Miriam, and to little Mary and Elizabeth, their daughters. We worshipped with the large company they had assembled; we partook of their hospitality; we slept in their compound. We saw and felt in their surroundings the influence of a Christian home.

It looks as though the Galilean had once more triumphed, and that against fearful odds. Christian marriage, even in Lango, is not quite so unfeasible as is sometimes alleged : " not with the help of God."

CHAPTER IX

Uganda's Gift to the Sudan

THE Sudan has a majesty of its own, a pathos of its own. The Sudan with its fifteen provinces, extending from Wady Halfa to Uganda, from the French Sahara to the Red Sea, is a world within a world, a continent within a continent. Its majesty is written in its vastness, its beauty, and its great potential wealth. Its pathos is written in its peoples. Comprising 984,000 square miles, it might well support 50,000,000 inhabitants. It has, however, a population of but 3,500,000. From the days of the pyramid builders to the day of its deliverance (2 September, 1898) at the decisive battle of Omdurman, it has been the quarry successively of Pharaoh and Khalif, Mameluke and Khedive, for slaves, ivory, and gold. "The Times" thus summarizes an article by Sir Ernest Wallis Budge :—

> The story of the Sudan is very long, but it is also very monotonous. The gist of it is that from first to last the Egyptians never really conquered the Sudan, or even any considerable part of it. Their

Uganda's Gift to the Sudan

alleged conquests were a repeated and interrupted series of raids for slaves and loot. One of these conquerors has himself recorded how he made war on the Sudanese. He ruined their harvests, fouled their wells, destroyed their plantations, carried off their women and cattle, and left their country a desert. He was a Pharaoh; but Mohamet Ali or Ismail Pasha might have made the same boast. Gold, slaves, and bribes were all that the Egyptians sought in the Sudan.

There are, it is true, two Sudans, the Arab and the pagan. Arabs completely displaced the Hamitic tribes on the Desert Nile in Nubia, Dongola, and Sennar after the eleventh and twelfth centuries, and in the last-named district, Sennar, founded the Funj dynasty of kings, which powerfully affected north-east Africa from the thirteenth to the eighteenth centuries.[1] The Sudan is still Arab to-day as far south as Kordofan; and in this Arab area there is, happily, small indication of an oppressive past. It is when south of Malakal you seek to make contact with the various clans of the Dinka or Acholi tribes (and these are principally the subject of this chapter) that you discover, in marked contrast to the Bantu races, how shy are these peoples to respond to any European approach. Bishop Gwynne tells

[1] " The Colonization of Africa."

a pathetic story of an old chief he met upon the Sobat River. "We are come," said the Bishop, "to be your friends. We have come to bring to you our Book and to speak to you of our God." "Sir," replied the old man, slowly removing his pipe and putting it on the ground at his side, "there came other men from the north who said: 'We have come to be your friends; we have come to bring you our book and to speak to you of our God'; and they took away our women, and stole our cattle, and made slaves of our children. Sir, we will wait a little." Australians of the Sudan United Mission, priests of the Austrian Mission, missionaries of the American Presbyterian Mission or of the C.M.S. have all the same tale to tell. They live among a people stricken and cowed by the sufferings and cruelties of their long, sad past.

Of the redemption of the Sudan this is no place to write. The redemption of the Sudan is a romance by itself, one surely of the noblest that our Empire can boast. Ismail, with all his callousness to Sudanese exploitation, was European at heart. In his desire to stand well with European, and more particularly British, opinion he sought the aid of British administrative ability, and to

Uganda's Gift to the Sudan 143

his famous Equatorial Province of the Sudan brought successively as Governors Sir Samuel Baker in 1869 and General Gordon in 1874. Baker had discovered Lake Albert in 1864; and in 1869, true lover of Africa, he returned at the head of an expedition for the suppression of slave-raiding that took him as far as Bunyoro, which was declared in 1872 to be a province of the Sudan. Gordon followed. He accepted the post from the Khedive under a compelling sense of mission. " They shall cry unto the Lord," had he not read of the Egyptians, " because of the oppressors, and He shall send them a saviour and a great one and He shall deliver them."[1] " I entirely take that prophecy of Isaiah," he said, " as my own and work to it as far as I can." His whole heart went out to the Sudan. As he noted the extreme wretchedness of its people he wrote : " What a mystery why they are created. Theirs is a life of fear and misery night and day. No one can conceive the utter misery of these lands . . . but I like the work, for I believe I can do a great deal to ameliorate the lot of the people."

As one stands to-day, forty years after, looking up at Gordon's statue outside the

[1] Isaiah xxix. 20.

palace gates in Khartoum, it is to reflect in what that supreme venture of faith issued. First, with its inevitable isolation and depression, so vividly portrayed by Mr. Strachey,[1] the governorship of the Equatorial Provinces; next the rule of the whole Sudan; then, after an interval of five years, the recall in 1884 to the forlorn hope, and the long, harrowing siege and death. It all seemed futile. But if ever seed bore much fruit it was Gordon's sacrifice. As he sits there above you on his camel, looking ever out toward the south, what is it that he surveys? Behind him is the beautiful palace reared by Kitchener upon the site of his own. Behind him too, the river, and the river war, and the thirteen years of solid preparation that ended in the victory of Omdurman. But before him? That is the great matter. Before him Wad Medani, and Sennar and Makwar, the mighty dam[2] and the desert—*his* desert—blossoming as the rose, with its cotton fields, like a sea spreading to the horizon, and a people transformed from terrorism to trust, partners with their administrators in one of the largest

[1] " Eminent Victorians " : General Gordon.

[2] The dam across the Blue Nile at Makwar is two miles long. It was opened by Lord Lloyd in 1926.

Uganda's Gift to the Sudan

agricultural schemes ever known.[1] Before him, still farther, Malakal, Bor, and Juba, with their growing zones of amelioration and education for the slowly recovering Nilotic tribes ; and Mongalla and Rejaf in his own Equatorial Province, starting-points to great highways leading right and left to the Congo, or to Uganda and Kenya, linking up the East African Protectorates into one organic whole.

There it all is, this product of Baker and Gordon, Kitchener, Wingate, and Stack, and that splendid corps of devoted administrators, soldiers, teachers, and missionaries who have worked with them. It is when we have eyes to see what they have given to the Sudan from the north that there becomes apparent—and not only apparent, but enthralling—what Uganda can give from the south. Already much has been accomplished.

The upward thrust from Uganda may be traced from a very early date. In a previous chapter the expansion westward through Toro has been indicated. It was about the same time (1895) that a northward development was begun in Bunyoro. For a long

[1] The Gezira Irrigation Scheme is designed to irrigate immediately 100,000 acres of cotton, and ultimately 3,000,000 acres. Of the profits, forty per cent are allotted to the native growers, thirty-five per cent to the Government to repay the loan, and twenty-five per cent to the Sudan Plantations Syndicate.

while the stalwart resistance of Kabarega, the Mukama of Bunyoro, had closed his territory to European influence, but with his capture and deportation changes followed. An active mission was founded by A. B. Lloyd. The Toro Church sent some of her best evangelists to help her mother country of Bunyoro, and by 1902 a big church had been built at Hoima, then the capital. Once again early fervour showed itself in evangelization. The Rev. H. W. Tegart led a party right out to Bulega in the Belgian Congo. To quote his own words : " The call of the dim, distant western hills across Lake Albert became unendurable and determined a call for volunteers." He left five teachers at five centres, and the work was subsequently taken over by the Africa Inland Mission.

More striking still was the missionary expansion from Bunyoro farther towards the north. A. B. Lloyd graphically tells how from the Nilotic people themselves came the first appeal for help. One day in 1903, when he was at Hoima, a wild-looking party presented themselves at his door. They had come from their chief, Ojigi, with a request that the Bunyoro Christians should send teachers to their country. Their petition was endorsed by the good Andereya, Mukama of Bunyoro. " These men have come from far away, from the great country called Gang to the north across the Nile. They are a warlike people, but their message is one of peace. They want to be taught about God . . . see these men then, my friend, and decide what you will do." To Lloyd such an appeal was irresistible. He responded at once. Not only did he quickly grasp the greatness of the opportunity, but he communicated his zeal to the Bishop, who hailed with joy this long-looked-for opening for Christianity in the Nile Valley ; and all who will may read in Bishop Tucker's vivid pages of the advent of the Gospel among the Acholi people. The Bishop, in company with Dr. and Mrs. A. R. Cook, spent Easter Day, 1904, in their midst. A. B. Lloyd was left in charge of the newly planted Acholi mission, shortly to be joined by A. L. Kitching. Lloyd built and evangelized ; Kitching with the help of an African colleague —Sira Dongo—tamed the rude Gang speech into writing, and within a year, incredible as it seems, he had a Gospel in their own tongue ready for the press. First at Patiko, then at Gulu, the work centred and grew, and so another post was planted to carry the current of the new power from Uganda into the Sudan.

From Khartoum similarly at this time the Church was endeavouring to stretch out a hand to these shy Nilotic tribes. It was not likely that a redemption of the Sudan inaugurated by Charles Gordon would consist only of material or social amelioration. During his lifetime he was in close sympathy with the work of the C.M.S. It was by his invitation that in 1879 the first reinforcements for the frail Uganda Mission came by the Nile route. He had expressed a strong desire that the Society should take up work especially among the tribes of that Equatorial Province of which he had himself been governor. When therefore in 1904 Lord Cromer offered the Society a definite sphere of work in this very area the offer was eagerly accepted, and in December, 1905, the Rev. Ll. H. Gwynne (now Bishop in Egypt and the Sudan) led out a party of six— F. B. Hadow, A. Shaw, Dr. Edmund Lloyd, A. Thorn, R. C. J. S. Wilmot, and J. Comely —to found the Gordon Memorial Mission in the Southern Sudan.

The sphere allotted to the Mission lay between the Sobat River and the border of Uganda, partly in the Mongalla (the new

Uganda's Gift to the Sudan 149

name for the Equatorial) Province, partly in that of the Bahr-el-Ghazal. First at Melwal, near Bor (1000 miles south of Khartoum), then at Gwalla and at Malek, the work was started. A new departure was made in 1912 at Lau, and in 1913 to the south-west at Yambio. Yei was opened in 1917. Dr. and Mrs. K. G. Fraser have since begun a most promising medical mission at Lui, and the Rev. H. F. Davies made what may be called a definite connecting-link with Uganda at Opari. In 1920 the Rev. C. A. Lea-Wilson, at the repeated request of the Sudan Government, initiated the first attempt in the way of higher education at Juba, close to Rejaf on the Nile.

It is only upon a personal visit to these lonely mission stations in the sub-Sudan that one can estimate the appalling difficulties that have been faced. Added to the great heat, a stifling breathlessness in the air seems to sap all energy, and the desolate flats offer no variety of outlook to the mind. But far hardest for the missionary is the elusiveness of the population and their extreme reluctance to permit contact, even when they are to be found. Sometimes for months at a time in the rainy season the low-lying lands become flooded, and the people may migrate out of reach of the Mission altogether. And, as stated above, long ages of misrule have left an entail of suspicion and fear.

Consequently two impressions are left upon the mind. First, that if education in the pagan Sudan is to be seriously attempted it is through Christian missions alone that it can be done; and second, that if these Nilotic tribes are to be won to civilization and to Christianity it will be through some upward thrust of native Christian influence from the south.

Has the Acholi mission in Uganda as yet borne fruit? Is it ready to spread northward into the Sudan? Has the early promise of this effort among these Nilotic tribes been fulfilled? It might be that in this more backward world the progress of Christianity might long be stemmed by the forces in league against its advance. While the Bantu experiment succeeded, the Nilotic experiment might fail. The thin line of European workers has been sorely interrupted and attenuated. The year of jubilee for the whole Mission, the coming-of-age year for this Gulu outpost, may well be a time for taking stock.

Uganda's Gift to the Sudan

Once again it is good to testify to what I myself have recently seen and heard. Few memories are so full of happiness as those that are associated with this Acholi mission. The journey involved, to begin with, a cruise of two days upon the Nile. True, this is not the Nile of Egypt, of Luxor or Assouan, the Nile of tombs, temples, and palace hotels. It is the Nile of papyrus, of hippopotamus and crocodile. Still, as you sit upon the trim little upper-deck of the " Speke," her stern-wheel tossing spray within a yard of you, it is to find the same spacious reaches, the same stately breadth of stream, the same inimitable cupolas in the cloud-land overhead, the same warm, embracing sunshine, the same stimulating breeze—in a word, the same charm.

To visit Gulu was therefore on each occasion something of a diversion; and Gulu itself fully justified this agreeable preface. The work at Gulu owes an immeasurable debt to the men who have led it—to Lloyd and Kitching, Fisher, Lees, and Lawrence. Their ministry, however, has not been continuous. In the inevitable intervals the mission has been in danger, and it is due to H. W. Tegart that after the first leaders had been withdrawn his head teacher, Sira

Dongo, was sent there from Masindi in 1910. Sira is one more of our missionary heroes in the native ministry. He it was who, coming to the leaderless, and in many cases lapsed, Christians of the place weaned them back from their bad ways, and by strength of character rallied and restored the infant Church. On my first entry, amid that welcoming concourse, such as is seen only in Africa, I must confess to feelings of a special reverence when I met this man at the head of his flock.

How can one estimate the state of an African mission? It becomes more and more difficult. Here among all these Nilotic people in the three districts Gulu, Lango, and Kitgum, each equipped with four or five British government officials (from Oxford and Cambridge chiefly), the Anglican Church had in my time but one clergyman, the Rev. Philip Lees. Ably he superintended his three widely-separated areas, each with some thirty or forty little congregations, and ran a boarding school, dispensary, bookshop, and office, to say nothing of a teachers' training centre. Yet, notwithstanding such lack of helpers, on my first visit I confirmed 158 (145 males and 13 females), I inspected a well-run boys' boarding school, and was aware of just those signs which speak of life.[1]

Sometimes it is some personal note that speaks more loudly than any tabulation of statistics. It was so in Gulu. Landing from the Nile, as I pressed on with Lees we met, some four miles inland from the river, a woman waiting by the wayside. One thing only was on her mind. "When," she asked, "can I have my Communion?" A wonderful question, surely, to hear in this remote land. "How many Christians," said Lees, "are there in this village?" "Four only," was her reply. Alas, we could only say that we were very sorry; we must hasten on; but there would be a celebration at Minakulu, twelve miles away, next morning at 6.30. It was a dark night, and an African dreads the darkness, because of the leopards. It was a wet night, and an African hates the rain. But there next morning, among the first six to come up to the rude communion-rail, was this poor Nilotic woman who had trudged the long twelve miles through the darkness and through the rain to receive the grace of her Lord in the way she craved.

[1] In 1926 Bishop Willis found 577 candidates awaiting confirmation in the Lango and Gulu districts—one proof of the continued development of the work:

L

Travelling northward again, from Gulu to Kitgum, our first night out was at Payira. Here we were the guests of a chief called Yona Odida, and remarkable was his story. Baptized some eight or nine years previously, he had fallen back into bad habits. Though married to a Christian woman, Yoniya Lawino, he took five pagan wives and began to share in heathen dances, and dragged down with him many in the countryside. Now by a sincere effort of will he had given up his evil life and was reunited to his wife Yoniya. Not only this, but by his decision he had brought back his companions with him. There was something truly striking about this man and his wife. His was the only house of a native in which I actually slept. Next morning the confirmation in the village church opposite his house, when seventy-two were confirmed, was something to remember. Such is the Nilotic character when touched by the Spirit of Christ. And is not this precisely the gift of lasting worth that these northern Nilotics of the Uganda Protectorate may bestow, if rightly shepherded, upon their scattered brethren in the Southern Sudan ?

Already even in these Nilotic regions the onward march of Christianity is to be seen

Uganda's Gift to the Sudan 155

on many sides. Gulu, Lango, and Kitgum have each some thirty to forty little congregations. These will soon, please God, increase and spread outward and northward. In 1915 a band of twelve young men from Uganda volunteered for work in the Southern Sudan. Nobly they have prepared the way. Soon we hope across the lonely wilds of the borderland there will advance that indefinable contagion to which we give the name of mass movement. The Acholi people themselves may infuse the irresistible desire to share this living, larger life of human betterment. The little bush school, the reading-sheet, the teachers' craft will do their work—and to the Church will be given the ducts and channels by which the greatest life of all may flow.

The new communications will help. But a while since the seventh cataract between Rejaf and Nimule, in intercepting the navigation of the Nile, seemed to intrude a serious partition wall between Uganda and the Sudan. Only for the more energetic traveller, prepared owing to the heat to trek at night, was the way open. For natives no less than for Europeans the one hundred miles' walk presented difficulties in the way of common organization. Now a highway has been made through the wilderness. It is a common thing for motor-cars to pass from Kitgum to Mongalla, and the labour of days is changed into the ease of a shorter number of hours.

The training of Nilotic teachers will help. At Gulu already there is a teachers' training centre. As we have seen in the Report of the India Delegation, as we have proved on every front of the Uganda Mission, the chief hope of the mass movement districts lies in the training of native teachers. Nowhere can it be more important than in gaining the confidence of the tribes to the south of the Sudan.

What will help most will be the gathering up of the scattered congregations among these Nilotic tribes, whether in Uganda or the Sudan, into one composite Christian family; as one flock under one Shepherd; and we may well give thanks that on St. Peter's Day, 1926, they were formed into a new diocese. No single event could more worthily mark the Uganda jubilee.

In 1904 we saw A. L. Kitching, the young Cambridge graduate, settling down among this Acholi people. Well may his heart rejoice that he who first gave to these children of the African wilds the Holy Gospels in their own speech should be called to be their Father in God, and to build for them in fuller measure the Kingdom of Him of Whom these Gospels speak. Well may we who have ever felt the appeal of Africa raise our thanksgiving for this new diocese of the Upper Nile, and pray that upon these long-parched peoples the river of life itself may flow, in the sure confidence that " everything shall live whithersoever the river cometh."

CHAPTER X

ADVANCING ON OTHER FRONTS

LIKE the spokes of a wheel the great roads for which Uganda is notable run out from Kampala, east and west, north and south. Like the segments of a circle thus connected with its centre are now to be found those outlying missions to which this jubilee pays tribute. For fourteen years the frail Uganda Church clung to the capital. Pioneer work began in 1891, when F. C. Smith went to Busoga and R. H. Walker to Budu. In 1893 Singo was occupied by Fisher and Kyagwe by Baskerville. From these first beginnings sprang that wide missionary expansion of which we have just read. We have seen how Christian influences began to be felt in Toro to the west and Bunyoro to the north-west; and how, from Bunyoro, Bulega was reached west of Lake Albert and the Acholi Country beyond the Nile. Eastward from 1900 we have watched the advances of Christianity in Elgon, Teso, Kitgum, and Gulu, and northward into the Sudan. It remains for us to

Advancing on Other Fronts

acknowledge what has been accomplished at either extremity, on the east in Kavirondo and on the south-west in Ankole and Ruanda.

Kavirondo is a large district to the south of Mount Elgon, inhabited in part by a Nilotic people, called Luo, in part by Bantus of the Bagishu type. Though now, by a later delimitation of boundaries, in the colony of Kenya and in the diocese of Mombasa, Kavirondo owes its first Christian instruction to Uganda. In 1905 the Rev. J. J. Willis, now Bishop of Uganda, entered the country and, touring round it, secured the sons of some of the Luo chiefs for his school at Maseno. Here Mr. H. O. Savile joined him, and under his direction a strong industrial centre quickly developed. In 1912 the late Archdeacon Chadwick opened up work among the Bantu peoples at Butere, where his sister, Miss J. E. Chadwick, with the assistance of Miss E. B. Downer, in later years exercised a wide influence over the women of the district. The Kavirondo mission has a striking record. From its perch high above the Great Lake, on slopes that lead by pleasant gradients to the Nandi plateau, many thousands in the country around have been influenced. Chief in maintaining the traditions under which the mission was inaugurated, have been Archdeacon Owen, F. H. Wright, J. Britton, and F. H. White.

Ankole, lying to the south-west, is the cattle district of the Protectorate. It is the home of the ancient Bahima tribe that has given to Uganda its four paramount chiefs or kings. Bishop Tucker visited the country in 1899, and the following year the Rev. J. J. Willis, then newly arrived in Africa, was sent there. Thirteen small out-stations were soon in existence, and the work grew with amazing rapidity. On 7 December, 1902, the king was baptized, also the katikiro and eighteen others. For the last ten years the work has been supervised by the Rev. H. B. Lewin, assisted by others at different times, and it has continued to grow apace. Here it was that with much effect the Boy Scout movement was first introduced into Uganda by H. M. Grace.

It is, however, with Ruanda, as the youngest child of the Uganda Mission, that this chapter must be chiefly concerned.

Ruanda lies beyond Ankole on the south-west frontier of Uganda. It is divided into four counties, whose names read like those from some fairy-tale : Rukiga, Bufumbira, Ruzumbura, and Kinkizi. Rukiga, with its hills, towers over the hot, steamy Ankole plains. Its green ravines stream with water. Bufumbira, that part of Ruanda that is under the British flag, possesses perhaps the grandest view in all Africa. Here the moon slips over the waters of five lakes, and great clouds leaning earthward spill themselves into grey craters on the lava plain below. Away to the west the volcano Namlagira flings into the night its flaming fires, while Muhavura dominates the scene, its sides scored deeply with mighty caves, and its long slopes inhabited by weird gorillas. Kinkizi and Ruzumbura are counties of drowsy, pasturing hills, the first richly wooded and rolling gently down to Lake Edward, where all day long the hippopotamus wanders at will and at night thousands of white pelicans travel over its lonely waters.

If its land is fascinating, so certainly are its people. From the aristocratic Batusi the scale descends to the pygmy Batwa tribe, swinging like monkeys from branch to branch of the forest trees, and dropping their spears on their prey as it slinks along the path below. The Bakiga, with their laughing, blunt ways, tirelessly dig and plant their crops over the countryside—a passionate, hard-drinking people this, whose strength of character stands out as something unique among the lethargic tribes of Central Africa. Here, too, are the Bahutu serfs, an agricultural people, and the Buhundi, who all day long fish in the lake and at night sleep in their little huts along its shore.

Such was the country and so were the people when in 1908 two schoolboys, the one from Harrow and the other from Winchester, met on their first day at Cambridge. They were both studying medicine, and they became firm friends. While at the University they resolved to use their medical knowledge in some unevangelized country in Central Africa. In 1913 they went to the northeast of the Belgian Congo, and in 1916 explored the east, centre, and north of Ruanda. Here truly was their "Land of Promise." After many difficulties and delays, the Ruanda Medical Mission was founded, and the two saw their dream coming true. On 11 February, 1920, the C.M.S. General Committee resolved "that the location of Dr. A. C. Stanley Smith and Dr. Leonard E. S. Sharp to Ruanda be approved."

Advancing on Other Fronts

They selected Kigezi for their centre, and built their station on the bluff running out into the great valley. Bit by bit buildings were planned and completed. The first patient was admitted into hospital in June, 1922. The dispensary work was taken over by Miss Watney, who had already done fifteen years' work in Mengo Hospital. By 1923 they were teaching the new religion of love by word and deed to over 700 in-patients alone.

"They are simple as children," wrote one of the doctors, "and every thought has to be presented to them with endless patience and repeated time after time." Yet quickly the light began to spread. The chiefs of Bufumbira came forward and offered to build a school for their own sons, and this was put up in 1921. In 1922 another was opened at Kabale; in 1923 yet another at Rukiga, and the first school for girls at Kabale, and still the movement grew. It is teachers and more teachers now that are wanted. Outside help will never be enough, though Buganda, Toro, Bunyoro, and Ankole most generously send what they can. In Rukiga alone there are already forty tiny native churches built by the people themselves. In Kinkizi the chiefs and readers have pooled their cash and their energies and built a church to hold 300 people. There are now 150 churches in the district.[1] From everywhere comes the clamour for leaders, and they must be trained. Who is to do it? There are very few native leaders who have reached the stage where they can guide others. They are children still, but they are the only stuff available, and so Dr. Sharp, travelling in Kigezi in November, 1925, is obliged to write sadly: " Among all the churches in this country there seemed to be only one teacher who could be regarded as an outstanding leader." Other stories filter through of a master here who has made moral shipwreck because there was no stronger human hand near enough to help him in his evil hour, and of another there who is having a bad influence on the boys of his school. This is the anxious side on which the shadows cluster.

But, in spite of much that is baffling, the work creeps forward. Along the eastern frontier stretches the line of Christian Churches; they form strategic starting-points for the rest of Ruanda, Urundi in the

[1] See Bishop's Charge, 1926.

Advancing on Other Fronts 165

Congo, and Uha in Tanganyika Territory. It is almost impossible to imagine what the needs and the demands will be in a short time, and what kind of a new world Ruanda may become.

CHAPTER XI

UNDER THE RED CROSS

WHEN Jesus Christ was on earth nothing could have been plainer than His intention for His earliest agents. " He sent them to preach the Kingdom of God and to heal the sick." " He ordained twelve that they should be with Him and that He might send them forth to preach and to have power to heal sicknesses." The preacher and the healer if not, as in their Lord's case, to be one and the same person, were at all events to go hand in hand. It takes time for the Church to perceive her Master's behests. She has been slow of heart to grasp many aspects of His teaching on human brotherhood and social service. She has only fitfully understood her healing function. Even in so obvious a field as that of the C.M.S. the year 1885 was reached before a Medical Auxiliary Committee was even planned. And in the Uganda Mission twenty years had elapsed before settled medical work was begun at Mengo in the year 1897.

Remarkable is the progress in the ministry

Under the Red Cross 167

of healing to be since recorded. Of Mengo Hospital we have written in an earlier chapter.[1] Let Dr. Albert Cook, its founder, give us some of its latest statistics. " The hospital," he writes, " is now in its twenty-ninth year, and the writer and his wife have been privileged to watch over the work from the completion of the first little reed sheds with thatched roof in the spring of 1897 to the present imposing mass of buildings which adorns the slopes of Namirembe Hill." In one single year the doctor now records :

>   In-patients . . . 2,069
>   Out-patients' attendances 22,589
>   Beds 180

In close proximity upon the western slope of Namirembe is the Lady Coryndon Maternity Training School, the product of the fertile brain of Mrs. A. R. Cook, M.B.E. Its objective is nothing less than the saving of the child life of Uganda by providing trained midwives for the whole country and by offering a maternity home for Uganda mothers in their hour of need. Urgently was such help required. In spite of immense difficulties, the results have been

---
[1] Chapter III, pp. 67, 68.

remarkable. For a recent year (1924) the figures are :—

No. of students	22
No. who passed government exam.	13
Total no. of in-patients	1289
Total no. of maternity beds	42
Births	596

But this is by no means all. To each of these institutions are attached respectively a number of branch dispensaries and country centres. At Iganga, Ndeje, Mityana, Bamusuta, Nakifuma, and Mbarara the outpatients have aggregated to another 33,000, while the country centres account for no less than 44,400. Mengo Hospital is thus an immense organization operating far and wide. Well does it merit the tribute accorded in the Phelps Stokes Report :—

> One of the noblest records of work in the whole of East Africa for the benefit of the community is that of the C.M.S. hospital in Mengo. . . . The hospital, opened in 1897, was the pioneer in medical work in the Protectorate. It has ever since held the lead, in introducing vaccination for smallpox and in notifying the first case of sleeping sickness. . . . The hospital has also done pioneer work in the medical education of the native. . . . The Lady Coryndon Maternity Training School is doing, under the direction of Mrs. Albert Cook, M.B.E.,

a splendid work in training the native women as midwives. In view of the terrible infant mortality in Uganda, caused by ignorance, dirt, and venereal diseases, the contribution made by such medical work to the welfare of the Protectorate is incalculable.

Given, then, this immense organization centring at Namirembe and branching out into so many outlying districts, it might well seem that the Church might rest content with so considerable a contribution to the medical work of the Protectorate. Not so. Upon the remote circumference similar daughter hospitals are rivalling their mother, each in a strong strategic position of its own. Reference is made elsewhere to those in Toro and Kigezi.[1]

Last but not least, under Dr. E. V. Hunter, aided by the liberality of Mr. Ernest Carr of Carlisle and Nairobi, our fourth big missionary hospital is coming into being at Ng'ora to serve the large population upon the cotton fields of Teso. Once again figures speak for themselves. They testify to the human hunger for the doctor's aid. In 1921, after much discussion, this Ng'ora centre was accepted on the advice of Major C. A. Wiggins, C.M.G., then Principal Medical

[1] Cf. Chaps. IV and X.

Officer for Uganda. In 1922 Dr. Hunter arrived on the scene. That year he and Major Wiggins operated under a tree upon a woman whose leg was bitten by a crocodile. For months his operating theatre was a mere hut. Yet from the first, as the numbers show, patients crowded in daily.

1922	Out-patients	11,636
1923	Out-patients	22,048
	In-patients	300
1924	Out-patients	33,862
	In-patients	820
1925	Out-patients	46,223

Slowly the new hospital buildings grew. Now there are two bungalows for the staff, an administrative block 80ft. by 30ft., two wards of thirty beds each, an Indian block of three wards, a dispensary, and a waiting room. For three years Dr. Hunter was surgeon and physician, architect, builder, and financier, all in one. Nobly Mrs. Dillistone, who before her marriage had worked at Mengo Hospital, assisted him. In 1925 a full-time nurse and a woman doctor came to his aid. " No fame or pleasure or wealth or power can compare with the joy of tending these

Under the Red Cross

sick ones or of trying to bring them to the Saviour of sinners and the loving Friend of the sick." So writes Dr. Cook at Mengo. Dr. Hunter at Ng'ora would say precisely the same.

It is scarcely, then, remarkable that the East African Commission should pay some tribute to a system of mission hospitals at once so widespread and so effective: " Uganda stands pre-eminent among the East African territories in the matter of the provision of medical services and hospitals for the native population. . . . A thousand pounds is a paltry sum to provide out of a total medical vote of £133,000, and we recommend that it be supplemented immediately out of revenue. Every mission hospital is creating an asset of great importance to the colony, namely, a class of men and women capable of taking charge of dispensaries and maternity centres."

It is this medical vote of £133,000 per annum that affords some idea of the Government's contribution to the health of the Protectorate. Only when one is actually on the spot is it possible to estimate the kind of solicitude that our Colonial Office entertains for the physical welfare of its dominions. In the case of Uganda each district, in theory, has its medical officer. In practice, working medical officers are stationed as a rule at Entebbe, Kampala, Jinja, Mbale, Soroti, Mbarara, Masindi, Bombo, Gulu, and Lira. While the Mission has eight doctors, the Government has fifty-three. According to the present Governor, " the volume of government medical work among natives in Uganda exceeds that of any other tropical possession."[1] It is true to say that mission hospitals were among the first in the field. It is true to say that the ministry of European women as nurses in these hospitals, whether Anglican or Roman Catholic, has up to the present given them an atmosphere and a fragrance with which no government hospital for natives can for a moment compare. Make, however, what reservations you may, no one can stay long in Uganda without appreciating the kind of gift made by the Government Medical Department to the general welfare. The results of medical work in Uganda are strikingly evident in the figures recently given by Sir William Gowers. The death-rate for 1925, 19.24 per thousand, is the lowest recorded for the country. The birth-rate of 27.4 per thousand is the highest,

[1] " The Times," 8 July, 1926.

while the excess of births over deaths represented an increase in population of 12,647.

Such tabulation of statistics is, however, as Dr. Cook says, "the mere bones of a living work." Enter some Sunday morning the largest of the native wards in Mengo Hospital and see for yourself what medical missions stand for. A number of beds drawn into a circle form, with their blankets, a crimson background. Within this enclosure a company of other patients crowd the floor. At the centre is the doctor in surplice and scarlet hood, himself the pastor as he is the physician of his flock. Direct and homely are his words : direct and homely the hymns sung. Or pay a visit, over the way, some week-day to the training school. The training of native hospital workers has always been in the forefront of mission policy. Mark the eagerness with which these African students trace the anatomy of the body or examine the analysis of human blood. Look in, as you journey through the forests of Busoga, at the little hospital at Iganga and discover what one tireless woman is accomplishing (for this is scheduled only as a dispensary) not only for the wasted forms in bed, but for the string of out-patients that here, as everywhere, forms such a prominent feature of hospital work. See for yourself the number of out-patients far away at Ng'ora, and try to imagine not so much what this long procession of 45,000 a year may mean to this solitary doctor, but rather what it may mean to all that broad countryside in the way of relief and healing and newness of mind.

The need for our Lord's great healing commission is blazoned afresh in all this revelation of pain and suffering such as only Africa knows. We may well give praise for our doctors and nurses who day and night are exercising their healing art in that hungry land.

CHAPTER XII

AFRICAN EDUCATION

No event in the development of native races in Africa has of recent years been more arresting than the publication of the Memorandum Cmd. 2374, 1925. This memorandum, emanating as it does with the imprimatur of the Colonial Office, declares:—

Government welcomes and will encourage all voluntary educational effort which conforms to the general policy. Co-operation between Government and other educational agencies should be provided in every way. . . . Education should be adapted to the mentality, aptitudes, occupations, and traditions of the various peoples, conserving as far as possible all sound and healthy elements in the fabric of their social life. Its aim should be to render the individual more efficient in his or her condition of life, whatever it may be, and to promote the advancement of the community as a whole through the improvement of agriculture, the development of native industries, the improvement of health, the training of the people in the management of their own affairs, and the inculcation of true ideals of citizenship and service.

The fact that the Government thus welcomes and desires to co-operate with the school work of the missions constitutes at once a remarkable tribute to their past educational effort, and a challenge of the most searching kind with regard to the future. We may well ask therefore what has been the educational policy in Uganda during the past fifty years and what response may be anticipated to the new demands of to-day.

It is suggestive that so early, as in the apostolic age, the African acquisitiveness for knowledge should find expression. The Ethiopian inquirer might be found on any road in Uganda now. He is everywhere reading. Still in answer to the question: "Do you understand what you are reading?" the very words of Queen Candace's steward might come back in reply: "How can I unless some one shall teach me?" For centuries Africa was but a huge barrier to the navigator sailing to the East. For centuries men sought ingress into it solely for its wealth. Now those who are acclaimed as its trustees are conscious of a dual mandate, not only as to its wealth, but as to its peoples. And with the first dawn of this new sense of trusteeship has come the desire to meet the African's appeal for education.

African Education

In the story of the Uganda Mission every missionary has been in some fashion a teacher. We have seen Wilson, the lonely pioneer, gathering out of the jungle his circle of readers. Mackay we have watched as, surrounded by every embarrassment, he instructed the African in the rudiments of woodcraft and engineering. In the early years, everything was of necessity fragmentary. Bishop Tucker numbers the schools when he arrived in 1890 as six, and the scholars 454. It was in that—to Uganda—decisive decade of the 'nineties that organized education took its rise. Bishop Tucker was quick to perceive its importance. " The course of my story," he writes in 1898, " now turns to education, or, as it has been fitly described, character-making. For what, after all, is education but the moulding of the character in high and noble ideals ? " He tells us significantly that organized education began with the advent of women missionaries in 1895.

C. W. Hattersley, who arrived in 1898, planned a complete scheme of education for Uganda. To the little bush schools that sprang up everywhere with the first coming of Christian influences was given the name of " day school." Very crude and primitive, their sole apparatus a spelling-sheet and an occasional blackboard, they expressed the primitive aspirations. Herein seated upon the earth floor may still be seen any day a graduated series of dusky circles, irrespective of age, beginning with the solemn chanting of two-letter syllables and ending with the baptism class. Upon this slender educational substratum were superimposed " central schools," one as far as possible in each considerable centre of population. Their credentials lay in the possession of a trained teacher, and of sundry books and desks, paper and ink. Their dignity was in general supported by an adjacent clearing in the jungle containing goal-posts and indicating football. Third in the scheme was the " high school " : denoted by dormitories and a big school and a well-kept compound. A serious contribution this to the country's life and future, for here a British teacher is in charge. Here are the chiefs' sons and daughters in residence, and here is the first adequate opportunity for discipline and atmosphere.

On the boys' side the culminating effort is the King's School, Budo. The product in the main of two Cambridge men (H. W. Weatherhead of Trinity, and H. T. C. Weatherhead of Emmanuel), Budo school impresses the visitor as a remarkable achievement. Upon the summit of a hill ascended by long, sweeping curves, it presents, in strange contrast to its wild surroundings, a trim quadrangle, each intersecting path an avenue of shady trees, a big school facing the gateway, a chapel to the left, with dormitories, technical workshop, printing-press, etc., filling in spaces on either side. Two bungalows provide for the British staff. It is already a school with traditions. To be a Budo boy is a coveted distinction. Budo has sent out chiefs, head teachers, clerks, shop-assistants, printers, and mechanics in number. The Old Budo Boys' football eleven has a fine record, even against British teams.

Corresponding in some considerable degree to Budo is the girls' school at Gayaza. Here upon a hill some ten miles from Kampala Miss Thomsett began work among girls so long ago as 1895. Subsequently Miss A. L. Allen, ably assisted by Miss Janet Smyth and others, started the boarding school and brought it to a high standard. Its permanent value to the life of the Church and the Protectorate is to be argued by the character of the women that have been there. Many, from the Queen downward, are now the wives of leading chiefs. In the Young Wives' Fellowship, founded by Mrs. Baskerville and carried on by Mrs. Ernest Cook, they have kept touch with their school traditions. And it is from this circle, more perhaps than from any other, that a better tendency in the way of family life will spring.

These schools are the delight and the pride of the mission and of the people. You may sit some evenings at Kamuli in that peaceful hour before sundown, with the large crowd that have been drawn from all the countryside to the touchline of the school football ground, when H. A. Brewer's boys are to play the Old Boys of Kamuli High School. You may feel the tenseness and the friendliness of it all. Or you may drop in some morning at the technical school at Iganga or at Masindi. At the one you may see a table or a wardrobe in course of construction for some government official, or a set of desks, or even choir stalls for some neighbouring mission station. At the other you may watch tanning of leather, and the upholstery of arm-chairs in the latest " club " style. Or you attend a school concert, or a march past at Mengo, or a speech day at Iganga Girls' School, or you pass from class-room to class-room at Nabumale or at Ng'ora. It is all one. The spirit is the thing. It is the spirit of the school at its best, as we have breathed it in England after generations of experiment—the spirit of the team, of discipline, of local patriotism. And very remarkable has been the translation of it into the heart of Africa, both among boys and girls.

Thus much for the first phase. The number of scholars given by Bishop Tucker in 1890 as 454 is given by Bishop Willis for 1925 as 176,033 ! Truly among these backward races, as Mr. Kenneth Maclennan puts it, " the world is at school." It is upon foundations so securely laid that the next section of Uganda's educational fabric is to be reared.

In America, that home of big projects, there has arisen a great " Trust " for the welfare of mankind, bearing the name of its founder, Caroline Phelps Stokes. The trustees, all of them " profound believers in the power of education as a factor of civilization," having reported earlier upon the educational needs of the Far East and of South and West Africa, resolved on 21 November, 1923, to send a further commission to East Africa, to visit Kenya, Uganda, Tanganyika, Basutoland,

Swaziland, and Abyssinia. This Commission was led by Dr. Thomas Jesse Jones, and included Dr. Garfield Williams of the C.M.S., Professor Aggrey, himself an African, Major Hanns Vischer for the Government, together with other experts. Previously Dr. Anson Phelps Stokes and Dr. Jesse Jones had many conferences with Mr. J. H. Oldham of the International Missionary Council, Sir Frederick Lugard, Mr. Ormsby Gore, and the Archbishop of Canterbury. On 25 July, 1923, Mr. Ormsby Gore announced in the House of Commons the appointment of a permanent committee " largely as the result of " Dr. Jesse Jones's earlier reports, to advise H.M. Government upon educational affairs in British Tropical Africa. This committee consisted, he said, of Sir Frederick Lugard, Mr. Oldham, Sir Michael Sadler, the Bishop of Liverpool, and Sir James Currie, with Major Vischer as secretary. The Phelps Stokes Commission, therefore, that sailed from London for East Africa on 15 January, 1924, represented much more than ordinary educational opinion. It represented the very best thought both of Church and State upon contemporary East African problems. The Report may well constitute the ground-plan for educational

African Education

reconstruction in British Tropical Africa for many years to come.

The fortnight 10-23 March, 1924, was allotted to Uganda. With head-quarters at Kampala, the Commission visited the government school at Makerere and the schools of the C.M.S., the Mill Hill Fathers, and the White Fathers. Meetings were held too with the native chiefs. Of the work of the missions the Commission writes in terms of warm appreciation :—

> An educational system which branches out into the whole Protectorate has been brought into being in co-operation with the native chiefs, but without any supervision from the Colonial Government, and until recently without any financial support. It is an educational achievement of which missions can legitimately be proud. Considering that educational work began in the Kingdom of Buganda only thirty years ago, and that in some of the areas of most rapid development in the Eastern Province education was introduced only a dozen years ago, the progress is amazing.

But higher standards and broader treatment are now acutely needed :—

> With full appreciation of the services of the past, it is now generally recognized alike by missionary societies and Government that educational facilities must be enlarged, and better adapted to the needs of the native people.

Better education, as the Report affirms, is rendered imperative by the new wealth through cotton, the necessity for instruction in hygiene, the need of better leadership in community life, and the need of providing in the face of cotton planting for adequate food crops. In the words of the Commission, Uganda " requires the immediate reorganization of native education, not only to avoid a crisis in native affairs, but much more to take advantage of the striking opportunities presented to the Protectorate and its people." Two criticisms are levelled against the present system. " The type of education has been too exclusively literary." The missionary societies " have made practically no provision for agricultural education." In spite of the substantial beginning in industrial training made by Alexander Mackay, " it is sad that the technical work of the C.M.S. in Uganda seems rather to have fallen on evil days." The second omission is with regard to hygiene and health. Other features exposed to the Commission have been the hampering of the present work by meagre financial resources, and the lack of proper supervision. The Commission accordingly issues six recommendations :

1. The appointment by the Government of a Director of Education for Uganda.

2. The creation of an Advisory Board on Native Education to represent Government, missionaries, settlers, and native people.

3. Generous grants-in-aid, conditioned by the quality and quantity of the work done.

4. A system of supervision by both Government and missions.

5. A re-grading of all the schools into four groups.

6. A course of instruction in all schools on agricultural and sanitary subjects.

It would be difficult for any commission, however able, to survey in the space of one fortnight, and with the various limitations of African travel, all the activities of Christian missions so widely ramified as those in Uganda. And it is open to question whether the existing Report has done justice to technical work. When I asked the manager of a big brickfield near Kampala how in the first instance he had got his skilled workmen, his immediate reply was : " We got them from the missionaries." When I complimented a government official on the excellence of his arm-chairs his answer was similar : " I got them from one of your missions." The Christian mission of to-day is like the Benedictine abbey of old. It is the great industrial, agricultural, and medical educator. It is when you see the burnt-brick churches that have been built, the ploughs introduced, the loom set up, the furniture made, the papers printed, the afforestation undertaken, the wheat grown and milled, the leather tanned, the ropes twisted, the baskets woven, the linen embroidered, under the direction of a small handful of white men and women that you realize that now, as in the Middle Ages, the industrial pioneer in a virgin field is still the Church.

Furthermore, it should be said that the first three of the Commission's recommendations merely confirm certain provisions that have for some time either been advocated or adopted by Government and mission conjointly. The new features are the increased supervision, the re-grading of the schools, and the systematic teaching of agriculture and hygiene. The spirit in which the whole of the recommendations have been received is proof of the general educational zeal. And the approval of the Colonial Office to this co-operative scheme, by which the State shall work as far as may be through the mission, opens a vista of extraordinary

African Education

hopefulness for the education of the Protectorate as a whole.

Now as to the staff! The Government offer with regard to education in tropical Africa constitutes a challenge of a most unusual kind to the whole Church. There is room for the expert who can take his or her part in framing educational policy, but the challenge comes very definitely to such as have contemplated the vocation of an elementary school teacher. For the terms "high" and "central" as used to describe schools in Uganda give an entirely erroneous conception of their standard and work. Both are lower elementary schools.

As to the response of women educationists, there appears happily to be little question. Organized education in Uganda, as Bishop Tucker chivalrously admits, began with the advent of the Englishwomen. Miss Chadwick at Namirembe, Miss Furley and Miss Thomsett at Gayaza, Miss Bird and Miss Pilgrim at Ngogwe, rapidly proved what could be done even in those early days. And from the first beginnings we have only to look to the outlying districts to-day to see what is being done by Miss Attlee in Toro, Miss Dorothy Smith at Nabumale, Miss May Gibbings at Ng'ora, Miss Salisbury at Gulu, Miss F.

Allshorn at Iganga, Miss Brewer and Miss Muller in Ankole. Of their work the recent Commission speaks in terms of unusual warmth. " On the whole it is difficult to give anything but praise to the women's educational work. A very small increase in their personnel would help them to put the girls' education of Uganda on to a very high level of efficiency." The ideal training-ground at home for the woman educationist in Uganda is the elementary school or the kindergarten. Already from such a setting some of our best have come. They start upon their work familiar with the organization and discipline of a well-managed school. To such this call from Africa comes with very special emphasis to-day.

With the men the case is somewhat different. The less-settled regime in the boys' schools, which is criticized by the Commission, is easily traceable to the circumstance that the clergyman in charge of a school may also have to be responsible for everything else on a station—agriculture, finance, transport, building, road-making, to say nothing of that which presses on him daily, the care of all the churches in the district. It is open to question whether the new educational proposals, together with the government offer that accompanies them, do not create a demand for a serious restatement of missionary service. The very word " missionary," so convenient professionally, is infelicitous in other respects. It obscures the lines of demarcation between the different vocations that have come to the aid of the Church overseas in recent years. We need to-day bishops, clergy, doctors, matrons, nurses, schoolmasters, schoolmistresses, school inspectors, accountants, engineers, technical instructors. Why not call them so ? Their professional work is in the main the same abroad as at home. Yet if they cross the Straits of Dover they are all classified as " missionaries," and the result, if unhelpful in other cases, is perhaps especially unfortunate as regards the new educational developments. A schoolmaster's work overseas is for many a young man a very fine field for service. In Palestine, in India, and in Ceylon the experiment of bringing men out direct from the Universities has been tried with satisfactory results. The time, it would seem, is ripe for a similar experiment in East Africa. No one wishes to minimize the difficulties in the way. It would have to be a fundamental condition that each man felt his vocation to be of the highest, and that each should work under the Bishop. The creation in such a way of a new avenue of approach to the present African needs would be widely valued. It would emphasize African education as being a great goal in itself. It would attract to its aid some of the best of our younger men.

One word in conclusion. Are we in danger in all this new development of subordinating the spiritual to the educational? There are those who gravely fear so. The Government, it is true, in their desire to conserve the spiritual element in African character, have on this account, as their memorandum plainly states, relied upon the aid of the missions. But the missions, in their earnestness to meet the government requirements, may tend to make the approbation of the inspector the natural goal to be attained. Nothing is more touching, under the present dispensation, than to observe in any one of the countless little bush schools which you may enter that the goal to be attained, as noted above, is everywhere the same. The object before all these dusky scholars is not to get a prize, not to get a job, but always to get baptized. However darkly, they are seeking first the Kingdom. This educational process is of the very essence of

Christendom in Uganda. Bishop Tucker says : " It must not be forgotten that the *first great essential* (as a Christian educationist understands it) is a knowledge of Christ, the Way, the Truth, and the Life, and that this has never been a subsidiary but always a primary aim of our work." Because no one might be baptized who could not read, therefore the school. Is it probable that under a government Director of Education, however friendly, the present order will remain ?

The time it would seem has come carefully to consider the desirability of establishing the baptism class outside the school system, after the manner of the confirmation class at home. It would be safer so for more reasons than one. By the Uganda Constitution those reading for baptism are exempt from labour for a period of six months. Perhaps in the early days this " reading " was, by contrast with their normal life, of the nature of work. By contrast with the busy life of to-day it is of the nature of unemployment. A class from 8 a.m. to 10 a.m. and all the rest of the day idle ! I once put to a whole baptism class of seventeen young men the question : " What work are you doing ? " And in every case the reply was,

"None." In view alike of the shortage of labour and of the moral value of work itself, it would be a positive gain both socially and personally if preparation for baptism were put outside of working hours. Such a policy might reduce the quantity of baptisms. It would, however, tend to raise their quality, for more effort and sacrifice would be called for from our catechumens, and the Church's position would ultimately be strengthened.

CHAPTER XIII

SOME PROBLEMS OF MIDDLE AFRICA

FIFTY years ago Uganda stood far afield from contemporary political or religious conflicts. Even on 30 October, 1886, "The Times" declared that "rival European ambitions for Africa do not reach to those remote recesses." To-day, as Mr. Kenneth Maclennan says, "For good or ill Africa has become an annex of Europe."[1] It is not surprising that, in a world that has experienced so swift an inrush of new ambitions, problems of the first magnitude should confront us, demanding infinite wisdom and restraint. Four that face every missionary at the present time are those relating (1) to the land, (2) to labour, (3) to Asiatic immigration, and (4) to the missions of the Roman Church.

(1) THE AFRICAN LAND PROBLEM

Of all factors in the making of a new Africa none exceed in importance that of equitable trusteeship with regard to land.

[1] "The Cost of a New World," p. 95.

Under Clause 22 of the Covenant of the League of Nations the humblest African takes his place in the world's scheme. The twenty-six clauses of the covenant form the first twenty-six clauses of the great Treaty of Paris 1919 ; and in Clause 22 it is expressly declared, first, that " the well-being and development of peoples not yet able to stand by themselves under the strenuous conditions of the modern world " shall form " a sacred trust to civilization," and, second, " that the best method of giving practical effect to this principle is that the tutelage of such peoples should be entrusted to advanced nations who . . . can best undertake this responsibility." It is not too much to say that for the African the primary test of the sincerity of this covenant is in the matter of his land. Abuses from which he has suffered are named in Clause 22. The slave trade, the arms traffic, the liquor traffic are specified. Not one of these, I believe, hits him so hard to-day as that one which is not named—the alienation of his land.

Africa has witnessed a successive number of efforts to solve the land problem. Swaziland, a Protectorate under the British Government, may be regarded " as one of the most amazing illustrations of the

Some Problems of Middle Africa

concessionaire evil."[1] When Lord Selborne endeavoured to bring some order out of the chaos, he found that every acre of land had been alienated to white men, and thus the native had nowhere to live. Basutoland, on the other hand, may roughly be described as a native reserve—that is, a territory within which white ownership is precluded. In South Africa in 1914, just before the war, General Botha introduced legislation to provide for an ultimate division of land between the races. It is, however, in Northern Nigeria that the highest example has been set. In the laws of Northern Nigeria, Vol. LXV, 1910, the foundation principle for African land settlement is declared. " The whole of the lands of the Protectorate of Northern Nigeria, whether occupied or unoccupied at the date of the commencement of this proclamation, are hereby declared to be native lands. . . . All native lands and all rights over the same are hereby declared to be under the control and subject to the disposition of the Governor, and shall be held and administered for the use and common benefit of the natives of Northern Nigeria."

Uganda by force of circumstances presents

[1] " Africa : Slave or Free ? " p. 121.

at the present moment two extreme policies in operation. On the one hand is the Uganda Land Settlement of 1900, the work of the commission presided over by Sir Harry Johnston. The ten years, 1884 to 1894, as shown elsewhere, were years of profound unrest, and in 1899 it became evident that the peaceful settlement of the new Protectorate could only be assured upon a satisfactory solution of the land problem. The first principle of the agreement is that the ownership of all lands " beneficially occupied " is vested in the native. All genuinely waste and unoccupied land became the property of the local administration. All that the Imperial Government asked was the " right of control " over about 10,000 square miles. This Uganda Agreement is looked upon as the Magna Charta of Buganda. But Buganda is one only out of the four provinces of the Protectorate. In outlying districts, some of them, like Lango, Teso, and Ankole, very prosperous, the land is " Crown land." These districts have been developed in quite recent years, and the very largeness of the provisions of the year 1900 for Buganda have militated adversely against native interests. In Busoga no African has a square yard to call his own.

The land problem therefore in the Uganda Protectorate is acute. " Why is our land now Crown land ? " I was asked by a native pastor in Busoga. " When through old age I cease to hold my chieftainship, where am I to go ? " inquired one of our senior Busoga chiefs. It is of the utmost importance to the making of a satisfactory future that an equitable settlement should be found, and it is for both Church and State to co-operate to this end.

For the Church the situation is generally much as it is for the natives themselves. In Buganda it is favourable. In the outlying districts it is very much the reverse. Under the 1900 agreement the Church received some fifty square miles, or 32,000 acres, properly registered. Some forty of these are located in the Province of Buganda, but by the prudent action of the Lukiko[1] ten were allocated by arrangement to outside districts—Bunyoro, Toro, and Busoga.

These " miles " are miles, it must be remembered, chiefly in the aggregate. They comprise a vast number of little plots, five, ten, twenty acres, given by chiefs in the early days of the Christian movement, and

[1] The word '*Lukiko*' means " a gathering of people at the headquarters of government." It is used here of the central council or parliament.

upon them, for its clergy and teachers, the native Church largely depends. Outside Buganda, more particularly in the Eastern Province, in Elgon, Teso, Lango, and Gulu, the Church must take up land under the Temporary Occupation Licence, or purchase outright any plots required for building churches and schools.

What then, both for Church and for State, for chief and for teacher, is the policy to press? We fall back with confidence to the note permeating Clause 22 in the Covenant of the Treaty of Paris—the note of *trusteeship*. We emphatically declare that no settlement can henceforward be acceptable which does not leave the land of the Protectorate in the hands of the authority as *a sacred trust*, first and foremost, for the benefit of the natives themselves. Native production has been proved again and again in Africa, east, central, south, and west, to be the secret of wealth. Native production will only permanently advance upon land in which the native, by personal allotment, has a direct interest. In Uganda, as in Northern Nigeria, let the Governor hold the land " for the use and common benefit of the native." It is under this head that the Church too will be rendered secure, for it is solely in the interest of the native that the Church holds its land.

One question remains. Does the trusteeship of the child race exclude the immigrant, whether European or Asiatic, from its scheme? Surely not. Africa suffers chronically, many affirm increasingly, from shortage of population. Upon the East African highlands, the European finds favourable conditions for a settler's life. Even in Uganda he can live for many years as a planter. How then shall the settler, both for his own good and that of his adopted country, best be accommodated ? By the policy of native reserves ? By the opposite policy (advocated by one far-sighted provincial commissioner) of *European* reserves ? By freehold estates ? There is much to be said against each and all of these proposals. The best policy yet put forward appears to be that of leasehold estates renewable every twenty-one years. In this way the planter secures access from time to time to better property, and the authority still in the best sense adheres to the principle of trusteeship.

(2) TRUSTEESHIP AND LABOUR

It is no slight indication of the public interest in the question of African labour that the " Labour Circular " of East Africa (1919) should have been followed by the now historic debate in the House of Lords (14 July, 1920) and by the weightily signed memorandum of the Archbishops of Canterbury and York the same year.

Nation after nation has witnessed the transition in the field of labour from the conditions of slavery or serfdom to those of voluntary work. In every case the transition has been slow, laborious, controversial. In many cases centuries have been required for its completion. The case of tropical Africa is unique in that it is only from Africa that slaves have been exported in any considerable number overseas, and only in recent times has this shameful traffic been abolished. Shortage of population constitutes one of Africa's chief problems, and is due in no small measure to the depredations of the slave-trader. The taint of slavery is still in various ways to be seen upon the people. All the more remarkable therefore are the changes that have already been introduced or sanctioned by British influence.

Slavery dies hard. It is as old as the human race. Slavery, though opposed to Christian principles, is not disallowed by

St. Paul. His respect for constituted authority perhaps prevented that. Though he restores the runaway slave Onesimus to Philemon " no longer as a bondservant, but as a brother beloved," he nevertheless does send him back, and, though the face of the Church has been set against slavery, it was only with the dawn of the nineteenth century after Christ's coming that Europe and America were prepared for its prohibition. Then it was as the initial and most essential measure that the export of slaves from Africa was condemned. Denmark nobly led the way in 1802. England under the persuasive efforts of William Wilberforce followed in 1806; America in 1808; Holland in 1814; and Spain in 1820. It was only in the middle of the last century that slave labour was abolished by other European states. England emancipated her West Indian and other slaves in 1833; France followed in 1848; and Portugal in 1858.

In Moslem countries, permitted by the doctrines of Islam, slavery still obtains; also in China in a modified form. But is all taint of slavery yet purged from our Empire ? " Certain peoples," says Aristotle, " are naturally free ; others are naturally slaves.

o

For these latter slavery is both just and expedient." The same view, as Sir Frederick Lugard pertinently observes,[1] has been held by able and influential men of our own day. To the African, they argue, owing to his lack of prevision and self control, such a state of dependence is not altogether distasteful; and philanthropic effort can best be directed towards regulating the conditions of slavery as a recognized institution. There is in the African situation to-day that which offers an inducement to regulate what is, in a veiled form, the condition of slavery as a recognized institution.

There is in the first place the labour shortage. With a native population of about 3,000,000 and a monthly demand for unskilled labour by Government and private employers for only about 15,000 men, it might naturally be assumed that in Uganda no labour problem should exist. But be it remembered that before any labour is available for hire certain debenture charges on the capital labour supply of the country must be met. Most important, of course, is the production of sufficient food for the native population. Inevitable, too, is the labour required to keep native huts and

[1] "The Dual Mandate in British Tropical Africa," p. 356.

roads in a state of repair. Third—and most considerable from the planter's point of view—is the energy expended by the natives in the cultivation of economic crops, of which cotton and oil seeds are the most important. These considerations, coupled with the disinclination of the African to any kind of non-compulsory work, produce even in the Uganda Protectorate (and considerably more so in other parts of Africa) a serious labour shortage, and very naturally incline planters and settlers to take such steps as they can to secure labour, if necessary under compulsory conditions. Forced labour, many affirm, should be regulated in the general interest of the community as a recognized institution both for public and private enterprise.

There is in the second place native custom. Among the people of Uganda two sources of forced labour have been available by native custom for many generations : those known as (*a*) *kasanvu* and (*b*) *luwalo*. Each of these is compulsory, or forced labour. Kasanvu is paid ; luwalo is unpaid. Kasanvu is paid at a low rate, about half that of voluntary labour. It is based on the hereditary right of the chiefs to call for labour for public purposes. Luwalo work, or work done in rotation has been the practice in the Buganda Province from time immemorial as a kind of general tax.[1] The national obligation to work for the common weal is recognized by custom and by the agreement of 1900, and the fact that the labourer is employed near his home and is able to return there at the end of the day goes far to compensate for any inconvenience involved. The agreement lays down that " the chief of a country shall have the right to call upon each native town, village, or commune to furnish labourers in the proportion of one man to every three huts to assist in keeping the established road in repair—provided that no labourer shall be required to work on the roads for more than one month in each year."

Bearing in mind these various considerations—the shortage of labour, the local traditions of forced labour, the innate indolence of the African native—it is not difficult to imagine the subtlety of the arguments that appeal to trader, planter, and even to missionary. The gathering of a crop, the development of an estate, the erection of a building, the shifting of material require immediate labour. What more natural than

[1] Report of Uganda Development Commission, 1920.

to solicit the influence of a chief or the more formal resources of the Administration? Private enterprise is essential to communal progress. Sturdy toil is beneficial to character. Some requital in the form of labour is the fit return of the child race for the benefits of which they are consciously or unconsciously the inheritors.

It is easy to picture the outcome of such reasoning. There is much in it that is expedient, if not salutary. Yet, withal, there must result the same lowering of the worker as under the earlier regime, and the same hardening of the employer. In a more progressive age there results also the widening rather than the closing of a breach, and the inculcation of a growing mistrust between protected and protector.

It is in view of these things that the dispatch of Lord Milner and the Memorandum of the Archbishops have come to the African with such saving grace. " It is of vital importance to us as a nation," say the Archbishops, " that we should have a clear and definite policy in regard to the administration of our African Empire which we know to be consistent with the principles of trusteeship. . . . We are bound, moreover, as a Christian nation to bring all national policies to the test of conformity with the Christian conception of the supreme value of human personality, and the worth of each individual in the sight of God. We cannot without the surrender of our deepest convictions reconcile ourselves to any policy in regard to the natives of Africa which contravenes this truth."

Negatively the memorandum is wholly against compulsory labour for private employers. " We welcome the assurance in the dispatch that there could be no question of entertaining any proposals which involve the principle of compulsory labour for private employment, and that such a policy would be absolutely opposed to the traditional policy of H.M. Government." Writing as one who was present at the debate in the House of Lords upon African labour, I can testify to the emphasis with which this principle was asserted by Lord Milner himself, that under no condition can compulsory labour be used for private ends, and to the cordiality of its reception by the entire House. No single dissentient speech was made.

Positively the signatories of the memorandum look to security of land tenure and steady education as factors in the requisite industrial improvement. " The principle of trusteeship implies the duty of fostering in all possible ways the growth of a healthy and independent life. This includes the assurance to the natives of adequate land, with security of tenure, and of complete freedom in the disposal of their labour, the furtherance of their economic development, their education in agriculture and industry, and a definite and progressive policy of training in responsibility and self-government."

It is one thing to write a memorandum. It is another to translate ideals as lofty as these into actual working in the midst of backward tribes. Yet the last generation has witnessed changes even in tropical Africa that are amazing. It was only on 2 July, 1890, that the Brussels Act for the suppression of the slave trade in Africa was signed. This Act, to which sixteen of the principal nations of the world were signatories, was a charter of liberty for the African slave.

One generation, and what do we see to-day ? Luwalo not abolished, but exemptions provided for by a properly organized commutation in cash to the State. The last time I was in Kampala I was struck by the excellence of certain new roads, and was glad to hear that these were entirely the outcome of the large income derived by the native Lukiko by commutation for luwalo.

And kasanvu ? Mr. F. H. B. Sandford, in his able "Notes on the Labour Problem," does not hesitate to testify that : " Kasanvu may be regarded as an open sore in our administration." Over and above its varied attendant evils is the inequality with which it presses upon minorities. " I know," he says, " that the Entebbe district labour registers for 1918–19 show that 72 per cent of the tax-paying population are exempted for some reason, and that 16 per cent escape the work in some way or other. The burden is borne by the remaining 12 per cent."

Much has been done to ameliorate the conditions of this forced labour. In Circular No. 26, 1921, it is expressly laid down that medical examination is necessary before men can be called out for it ; that there shall be allocation of duties according to strength ; that nine hours a day are not to be exceeded ; that labour will not be required on Sunday except in genuine emergency ; that labour shall be housed in weatherproof huts ; that on *safari* (journeys) there shall be a limit of fifty pounds per man, a limit of sixteen miles per day, and twelve miles on long safaris; that human transport is not to be allowed when mechanical transport is available. Local administration has furthermore raised the payment of porters from one to two florin cents per mile.

Still, with every precaution and every protection, kasanvu, or forced labour, must remain but an interim institution; and I know of no more conspicuous proof of the sincerity of British principles than that in 1921 in the province of Buganda, in spite of all that might be urged to the contrary, kasanvu was stopped.

Voluntary labour in Central Africa is a great risk, a great experiment. Pessimists are not slow to express their fears. For myself I have already seen that in the African which makes me sanguine as to his industrial future. I have watched the punctuality and the skill of the roadmaker or the gardener. I have noted the precision of the man at the wheel in the intricacies of the Kioga sudd; or the man at the steam-winch discharging with nicety his huge loads at Jinja pier; or the motor-boy's clever driving; or the carpenter's precision at his bench. But, of course this is but one side of the picture, as residents in Uganda speedily discover.

It is for the State to organize, for the Church to inspire. What of the Church's part in all this ? If it was Cardinal Lavigerie who preached a holy war against Moslem domination and the consequent slave trade in Africa, it was Bishop Tucker who stood out as the champion of the native's claim upon his land, and it has been from first to last the Christian missionary who has given the African ever fresh incentives in the way of voluntary production and voluntary work.

True it is that some familiar with the Uganda of a generation ago will be reluctant to part with the system of forced labour. Conscious of its convenience, they have read into it something approaching to philanthropy or, at any rate, to education. " Here," they have said, " is a scheme by which the child race might be put to the school of labour. Let it contribute out of the toil of its hands to the household of grace. Beware," they say " of precipitating the child prematurely into the freedom of the grown man."

Yet sometimes those at head-quarters see more of the battle than do the advanced troops. The appeal of the Archbishops, endorsed as it was by the heads of other religious communities, by members of both the Houses of Lords and Commons, and by many public men beside, lifts the whole issue of native labour to its right level and invests the African with his true dignity. The supreme value of human personality and the work of each individual in the sight of God, these to them are the fundamental conceptions. As we base the progress of the African upon these foundations we may face his future without fear.

(3) THE RACE PROBLEM

If the problems of land and labour may be claimed as belonging in Uganda to the sphere of domestic politics, there is a third which opens up more complex considerations. As we look across the world everywhere we see the rise, as Mr. Basil Mathews so forcibly reminds us, of "a stupendous tide of racial movement on the shores of humanity. . . . The white races that dominate the world to-day are faced by the clamour of the coloured races for a place in the control of the world."[1] Recent events have tested the force of this statement in East Africa. At the present time we find in Kenya about

[1] "The Clash of Colour," pp. 31, 160.

20,000 Indians, and in Uganda about 4000. The Indian is the retail trader. He is in East Africa what the Greek or the Syrian is in the Sudan. He hands to you in the remotest regions the products of Manchester or Cawnpore. On government stations he is prepared to offer you the amenities of life, such as tinned peaches, cigarettes, boots, breeches, petrol, and Mobiloil. Farther afield he sits on his haunches at the crossroads under a sheet of corrugated iron, the vendor of native requirements. I remember once, when I thought that I was quite at the back of the beyond, finding an Indian ready to sell me some Sunlight Soap.

It is the war, with its after-effects, that accounts most largely for the Indians' present demand for political status. The ratification of the Indians' position in the British Empire is to be found in the official Report of the Conference of Prime Ministers and Representatives of the United Kingdom, the Dominions, and India, which was held in London in 1921. The wording of the resolution dealing with " the position of British Indians in the Empire " is as follows :—

> The Conference while re-affirming the Resolution of the Imperial War Conference of 1918 that each community of the British Commonwealth should

enjoy complete control of the composition of its own population by means of restriction on immigration from any of the other communities, recognizes that there is an incongruity between the position of Indian as an equal member of the British Empire and the existence of disabilities upon British Indians lawfully domiciled in some other parts of the Empire. The Conference accordingly is of opinion that in the interests of the solidarity of the British Commonwealth it is desirable that the rights of such Indians to citizenship should be recognized.

It is scarcely surprising that a resolution of so weighty and so far-reaching a character, making its impact upon a situation already somewhat acerbated, should have produced, among Europeans and Asiatics in East Africa, feelings that ran high on either side. On the one hand, Indian expectation, fanned by an ardent nationalist press from Calcutta and Bombay, rose to anticipations of a political status which would have far surpassed the conception of the Imperial Conference as a whole. On the other hand, British feeling, naturally alarmed as to the consequences to which such pretensions might spread, stiffened solidly in opposition to the Indian claims. Europeans, it was seen, were in a small minority. England and England alone had made life possible and secure for immigration. England was responsible for the trusteeship of the native. Asiatic domination was unthinkable. What therefore might appear at first sight to be a purely local question assumed Imperial proportions, affecting the principle of " the solidarity of the British Commonwealth " and the integrity of the assurances given to the peoples of India.

In the face of such strangely divided counsels, what lead should be given by the Christian Church ? The Church is alive and vigorous both in Africa and India to-day. If it is not for the Church to dictate a policy, she should at least affirm certain principles applicable to the situation. First and foremost we must declare that the moment is one for large views. The view that we must keep steadily before ourselves is the Commonwealth of Nations, of which we should be the inspiring and unifying source. While we have the ends of the earth as our boundary, we cannot but entertain a holy jealousy for that vast tract of it that looks to us Englishmen, with our privileges and our inheritances, for influence and protection. The British Commonwealth regarded as one body must be the first charge upon our service and our ideals. The findings, therefore, of the Imperial Conference of 1921 constitute the sort of commonwealth charter which our Church should be the first to champion everywhere. Enunciated in a moment of high idealism, these findings may need stalwart support through more mundane days. The policy they outline may not be capable of immediate realization, yet it is a high point reached on the upward climb, and one to be stoutly held.

Starting, then, with the commonwealth view, we shall lay down as a second principle that within our Commonwealth those shall receive primary consideration in each land who are themselves its natural inhabitants. Here again the idealism of our statesmen at the Paris Conference in 1919 will find endorsement in the Christian consciousness. Under the famous Clause 22 of the Covenant of the League of Nations, the well-being and development of peoples " not yet able to stand by themselves " shall form " a sacred trust of civilization." How much more shall they form a sacred trust for those to whom they are peculiarly committed! The predominant concern of our African administration must be the trusteeship not of the Asiatic, nor even of the European, but of the African.

As an inevitable corollary to the foregoing, it follows that if this trust is committed to

British care, it cannot be abdicated by us, or delegated to others. I will not argue this point. The leaders of Indian opinion are at one, it appears, in disclaiming any desire to become responsible for the government of the native peoples of East Africa.

What, then, follows? In our desire as an Empire to do justice to the Indian, we have already accorded to him political rights. In the Legislative Councils both of Kenya and Uganda he has his place along with the European. In Kenya I understand that the Indians do not find fault with the number of their representation. By the system of election provided for in the community system both Europeans and Indians may elect separately their own members. In this way a sincere effort has been made to incorporate those Indians who are " lawfully domiciled " in Kenya in the administration of the affairs of their Colony. Similarly by the Settlement of 1923 the Segregation Order of 1920 has been rescinded.

The end is not yet in sight. For the moment in East Africa we are at the beginning—a critical and anxious beginning. At this juncture it is our duty (and this may be our special spiritual function) to call upon our Indian fellow-subjects, until a further stage in African civilization has been attained, for such a measure of trust and of patience as will meet this present position of affairs.

And while we have to make this request of our Indian neighbours—this delicate and difficult request for patience—we have another, as a Church, to make of our own fellow-countrymen.

" We have no Indian problem in Uganda," said an Indian barrister on 29 September, 1922, at the farewell to our retiring Governor, the late Sir Robert Coryndon, K.C.M.G. And when I asked him afterwards what he meant by his words he replied: " Our problem politically in Uganda is identical with that of Kenya in every respect. What I implied was that socially things are different here. We are here treated with consideration." The Indian is extremely sensitive, and he rarely forgets a kindness.

Africa has every indication of a great future, but at present, naturally, there is not enough business to go round. Transport is costly and many things are difficult. Everything depends on patience and good-will. Successful colonization here, as in other parts of the Empire, necessitates the co-operation of the various forces that are making for progress.

P

If at this important stage—this earliest stage of administrative experiment in Eastern Africa—either commercial rivalry or racial animosity is allowed to embitter the situation, then the necessary combination will be dissolved. The Britisher's brain-power, gifts of leadership, and stolid perseverance in the face of obstacles; the Indian's diligence, business capacity, and skill; and the African's physical powers, unfailing humour, and sterling worth—all are needed. If these principal partners in this commonwealth scheme can each continue with patience and forbearance to make his due contribution, we may look forward with sanguine expectation to a combined product in the next generation that shall far exceed anything as yet realized.

(4) AFRICA AND ROME

In every district in the Uganda Protectorate you will find to-day some representative of the Church of Rome. For example, at Kitgum, far to the north, one of the first objects to meet the eye is the large brick church of the Italian Mission. Here are a little company of priests, lay brothers and sisters, good peasant people from Verona. Here is Brother B——, bearded, smiling,

Some Problems of Middle Africa 219

kindly, and, above all, effective, rearing tier upon tier a brick church with transepts and apse, campanile and vestries, with naked Acholi labourers, who as they build have known no precedent for their building, have never seen such a thing in their lives before. Brother B—— is the smiling and kindly *fundi* (skilled workman) of the whole district, instructing the raw natives in simple handiwork, mending such vehicles as may convey chance Europeans to the place, spreading round him the first dawn of the artificer's craft. Here in Kitgum there is no C.M.S. missionary. Brother B—— and his companions stand in the eye of the Government for elementary technical training and effective settlement.

Father R—— is of another type—cleanshaven, English-looking, in khaki shirt and shorts. I first met him in the house of a Busoga chief. I thought that I had come on some brother clergyman of our own Church who was new to me. Father R——, however, is a Dutchman; he is one of the Mill Hill Mission, capable and quietly enthusiastic. A pastor at heart, he talked one day simply and sanely about the care of "the inner-man" in the African; remarked that we get about as much out of the

African as we put in, which, as he admitted sadly, was little enough ; declared that we can produce saints in Africa if we are prepared to face the cost of doing so. But Father R—— by occupation is an organizer ; he has got concessions on Thruston Bay, a bay on Lake Victoria that pushes up into the cotton region of Busoga. Here he has built a pier to which government lighters can be brought, and started brickworks and saw-mills, and obtained fishing rights. To the Administration he is a useful developer of a fresh marine base upon the Great Lake.[1]

Or, it may be, I recall Bishop F—— of the White Fathers—a Canadian, sunny and courteous, showing us with just pride the aisles and transepts of his fine cathedral, now completed upon the hill of Rubaga.

Or I remember Mother C—— of Kamuli, in her snow-white scapula, wimple, and veil, her knotted white cord denoting her membership in the Franciscan Order. Young, graceful, and kindly, she is a true product of our North Country. She comes from Manchester. She is devoted to children, to her hospital, and her roses ; but most to her little chapel. Here, she told me, six full hours of

[1] We much regret to note that Father R—— has since met death by drowning in Thruston Bay.

Some Problems of Middle Africa

prayer form part of each day's rule. She is a charming hostess. She lived when I met her in one of the very worst and most depressing districts, but all around her she spread a fragrance. You took knowledge of her that she had been with Jesus.

I could multiply instances. In every district you may meet these Roman missionaries—English, Irish, Canadian, French, Italian, Austrian, Dutch. Making every reduction you may wish, every concession to jealousy, prejudice, or misrepresentation that may suit your mood, the fact still confronts you that here is evidence of an immense missionary crusade. Here, whatever you make of its presentation, is Christianity in occupation and in operation. The problem is not domestic or racial : it is profoundly religious. What is to be our attitude as members of the Anglican Communion to these representatives of the Church of Rome ?

Our comparative indifference to the Romish question in England must not deafen us to the insistence of the problem overseas. Taking, for example, Equatorial Africa alone, the White Fathers' Mission, founded comparatively recently by Cardinal Lavigerie, has already some 600 priests at 120 different stations, grouped under eleven vicariates

And this is only one of the missions at work in Uganda. Two Roman cathedrals rise on opposite hills even in Kampala, the White Fathers occupying the western half of the Protectorate, the Mill Hill Mission the eastern part ; while the Italian Mission from Verona is in the north. In Uganda, according to the census of 1921, out of 1269 Europeans, 286 are tabulated as " missionaries," of whom close on 200 must be Roman Catholic. But it is not the number of Roman missionaries that is significant. In the vast spaces of Africa numbers are of small notice. What is everywhere arresting is the close approximation of the two mission stations. Sometimes wisely separated by a mile or so, at other places they are in close juxtaposition on the same area. At Butiti as I approached I found the two indistinguishable on the sky-line in the same clump of trees.

In earlier days an experiment was made in the direction of what is termed missionary comity. According to this principle, widespread in its operation between evangelical bodies, each missionary society will confine its ministration to a definite geographical area. The strong position of the Roman Catholics at Villa Maria in Budu (the Namirembe of the White Fathers) is a trace of this earlier experiment, initiated by the Government after the troublous years 1885-94. In the Sudan this policy of defining the spheres of missionary influence is still maintained. It is an obvious solution, yet one little calculated to succeed in practical working, for the plain reason that to the ultramontane theologian Protestantism is all one with paganism. To the Anglican all fields which lie beneath the British flag are presumably his to occupy. But to the experienced administrator religious toleration is by this time much too deep-seated a principle of Empire to be wisely disturbed.

Picture to yourself, then, the situation thus arising, and consider its effects. You have motored, it may be, some eighty miles or more through long grass or scrub, that conceals almost all vestiges of human occupation, to find on a sudden in this lone wilderness two stations, often, as I have said, in close juxtaposition. Each looks outwardly much the same as the other. Each, under thatched roofs of varying height and dimensions, has its church, its dispensary, its schools, and its dwelling-houses. Each has its acreage of cultivation and clearance, its roads and its plantations. And, in practical working, once this unhappy dualism has been set up there is, I think it must be confessed, little difficulty. Human nature seems seldom to postulate unity, rarely to be startled by schism. Each missionary contrives to go on his way either ignoring the other or fraternizing with the other, as the case may be. Once baptized, natives seem to adhere to their denomination as to their tribe. The administrative officers in their rounds call on each mission irrespective of its propaganda. Each is treated by the Government with equality. Between the two missions there obtains, I gather, little poaching, little friction.

It is in the field of religion that the difficulty chiefly occurs; and from the religious point of view the difficulty is so great that it is always challenging an answer. " Can it be right "—I quote the question in the words of a Belgian administrator, himself a devout Roman Catholic—" Can it be right to present to child races a warring element among Europeans in the presentation of their religion ? "

What is to be the attitude between these two world-wide forces—Romanism and Anglicanism ? What is the reason for their ever-growing expansion ? This is one of the most pressing of missionary problems. If

Some Problems of Middle Africa 225

past history has of necessity embittered rather than tempered the animosity between them, has modern philosophy, has the transformation of human society out of the Great War nothing different to offer ? If at the Vatican or at Westminster we must still be distant, must we be no other when we meet in the heart of Africa ?

Of the conventional attitude of Roman to Anglican there is still no question. The former is left cold. He feels no interest in the discussion. There is nothing to argue about. Of the conventional attitude of Protestant to Roman there is again no question. It is unthinkable ! *Rome* ! As soon compromise with the arch-enemy himself! But for a growing number the conventional attitude has faded. The old fear, the old shuddering, the old prejudices have been modified, and in their place has come a readiness to test the two missions by their results, above all to inquire into the question in a dispassionate mind. A young government official journeyed with me one day from camp to camp. He was full of the question. The son of a Free Churchman, his earlier associations were all anti-Roman. Yet Africa had given him to think. The Reformation he saw was necessary. It had to come. But Rome had changed since then in a measure, and, if only in a measure, still to-day out here he felt each had something to learn from the other. His attitude appears to be a general one. Government people, with a Church of England background, have a considerable liking for the "Fathers." Their staging, their ascetic poverty, their sociable ways all make an appeal. What is possible, what is impossible in the way of a new attitude to this age-long problem?

What is impossible is to undo past history. Uganda has its ineffaceable memories of past wrongs. What is impossible is to minimize genuine differences. Differences that have cleft asunder congregations, families, and nations cannot be minimized. What is impossible is for Christendom to unite under any Head but Christ. No earthly vicar, no terrestrial vice-regent, no human pontiff can be accepted in His stead.

What is possible is at least to let in more light and more love. Even to-day in this age of toleration each of these two vast ecclesiastical organizations stands veiled from the other in an almost impenetrable cloud, that seems only to lift at intervals sufficient to disclose each other's demerits. Rome's attitude seems to be one almost entirely of arrogance, ours of independence. What at least seems to possess the sanction of divine approval is that Christians, owning the same divine Head, should intelligently try to gauge each other's best output for the world's good.

CHAPTER XIV

Co-Trustees

IF the visitor to Uganda has garnered certain memories of a notable Christian mission, he is bound also to carry away with him impressions of a distinctly successful administration. From his first landing at Entebbe pier till his final exit, say at Kitgum, into the Sudan, his mind will retain a succession of gentle and agreeable surprises. The gradient of a road it may be, or the span of a bridge, the cementing of a culvert, or the lay-out of a cotton field, the turfing of a golf links, or the running of a ginnery—these have in turn caught his approving eye. He has not been surprised at the muddle of Africa. He has been surprised at the neatness of Africa. He will remember the bright patches that are illuminating the dark continent. He will think often of the chain of trim government stations wherein his spirit has been refreshed, each an oasis of order and kindly discipline in a primitive land.

Effectiveness is everywhere the note of government work, coupled with an unfailing sense of responsibility. The District Commissioner is head of his district. He knows it, and every one else knows it too. He may be on safari, in khaki shirt and shorts, but the royal arms gleam on his topi, and that is enough. *Govamenti* is a word spoken with awe. These government people, whether they belong to the Administration or to the Public Works Department, whether they are judges or magistrates, doctors or police officers, agriculturists or marine superintendents, are making a new world in British tropical Africa. No record of modern Uganda would be complete without some tribute to their achievement.

That which, however, a missionary desires rather to acknowledge is of a more personal description. Frequent acts of hospitality and of service to the mission form pleasant memories. Certain distinctive occasions linger agreeably in the mind.

I think of an August bank holiday, safeguarded quite as jealously in Africa as at home, when in one of our outlying districts the whole European community had selected as their rendezvous, for tennis tournament, football match, and tea, not the government station, not some planter's estate, but, as most popular and most agreeable, the mission station in that district. Every one was there —commissioners, P.W.D. officials, planters, ginners, even the portly Father of the Mill Hill Mission ! I recall a Christmas Day in such another outpost 400 miles away. All of the government circle but one (and he was accounted for) came up to the Mission for their Christmas service, and afterwards played tennis on the mission court. I think of a farewell dinner to one of the best of African statesmen—Sir Robert Coryndon—on his departure from Uganda. I remember, when the Provincial Commissioner was consulted as to the subject for an after-dinner speech, how quick was his reply : " Talk of the good relationship between Government and missions."

Fifty years ago the C.M.S. Mission came to Uganda, largely on the invitation of a distinguished traveller.[1] Twenty-five years ago, as the Bishop of Uganda reminded us in a recent charge,[2] " the Government came to Uganda largely on the invitation of the Mission."[3] Already in the interests of the British East Africa Company Captain (now Sir Frederick) Lugard had arrived in Uganda; and from the first he opened up friendly relations with the missionaries. Sir Gerald

[1] Cf. Chapter II, p. 19. [2] January, 1926. [3] Cf. Chapter II, p. 42.

Co-Trustees 231

Portal, the first actual representative of the British Government, followed his example, and from those early days until the present it has been this close association between the Bishop at Namirembe and the Governor at Entebbe, between the missionary on some remote station and the commissioner of his district, almost invariably friendly and frequently intimate, that has accounted for the reciprocity and understanding between Government and missions, and has been so distinctive a note in Uganda's development.

Certain considerations follow. We are inevitably looking ahead, and in the immediate future the mission on the European side must in all likelihood appear consistently as a small minority when compared with the steadily growing staff of the Government. " Where we have ten missionaries in charge of districts they have over sixty engaged in district administration; where we have a total male staff, clerical and lay, of less than forty they have over 400 ; while we can with difficulty secure a single recruit, they have at their call more men than they can employ."[1] What should therefore be the policy of the mission ? To maintain, as a first claim upon its staff, one

[1] Bishop's Charge, January, 1926.

resident missionary in each of the sixteen districts. Alike for superintendence of pastoral and educational work and for contact with the administrative authorities in his area; this one man would seem to be imperatively necessary to the upholding of Christian organization and Christian standards. He stands for something permanent and settled in the spiritual sphere. Church and State by virtue of the personal ties between him and his white confrères are saved from antagonism. Each is complementary to the other.

On the other hand, the time has now come for some closer incorporation of those in sympathy with the mission into its growing church life. The Church should be expressed less in terms of a mission, more in terms of a diocese. In every tropical country it is inevitably difficult for white and coloured to blend in any single ecclesiastical polity. Co-operation must in any case be carefully defined. The feelings of the African races quite as much as those of the European community must be sensitively respected. It is in consequence satisfactory that already the British congregations are represented by delegates in the Uganda Diocesan Synod. Already government officials and planters serve along with native leaders upon church committees. This co-operative principle so far admitted needs cautious yet persistent encouragement ; for out of it are important issues for the Uganda people in days ahead. Woe betide a Protectorate, such as that of Uganda, with its strategic position in tropical Africa and its unique history, if the growing wealth derived from its soil were to suffocate the true life of its people ; or if the growing ascendancy of those responsible for its administration were to blind them to the necessity for maintaining the religious life of the community at the highest possible level. The African is perilously susceptible to deteriorating influences. This is an hour in which old safeguards are crumbling and new temptations are surging in. It is therefore imperative that our government leaders should feel themselves to be co-trustees with those of the mission, not merely for the educational development of the native, but for his moral and spiritual welfare too. In this spirit of co-trusteeship lies the hope of our African dominions.

CHAPTER XV

FUTURE LEADERSHIP

"You sons of England, here is a field for your energies. Bring with you your highest education, and your greatest talents. You will find scope for the exercise of them all. You men of God, who have resolved to devote your lives to the care of the souls of men, here is the proper field for you. It is not to win numbers to a Church, but to win men to the Saviour, and who otherwise will be lost, that I entreat you to leave your work at home to the many who are ready to undertake it and to come forth yourselves to reap this field now white to the harvest." So wrote Alexander Mackay from the heart of Africa on 2 January, 1890—a few weeks before his death. Let the Uganda Mission in this hour of her jubilee blazon these words of her first great leader far and wide. For they carry with them, with Mackay's gift of eloquence, the message most needed by the Church to-day : " It is not to win numbers to a Church, but to win men to the Saviour . . . that I entreat you."

Future Leadership 235

The Uganda Mission has behind it a record that has again and again thrilled the whole Church. It has been the object of these pages to give some impression of the mighty product of these last fifty years at the heart of the African Continent. On the one side of this brief space of time you see swamp and jungle, on the other a land of roads and cotton fields; on the one hand sheer savagery, on the other an ordered social scheme; then paganism with all its superstition and its fears, now, in thousands of little centres the presentment, in however rudimentary a form, of Christian education and Christian worship. Behind all this, as the instruments by which this complex fabric has been fashioned, are the men and the women who have given of their life's best to this great end. " When I see," said Mr. Ormsby Gore, " what has been achieved in Uganda by our government officials, by our traders, and by our missionaries, I am proud to be an Englishman." In these pages an attempt has been made to show the debt of the Uganda Protectorate in this way and in that to this triple alliance. For the moment it is the spiritual arm of which I would speak. It is when, at such a time as this, the mind retraces something of the way by which this

Mission has been led, and recounts, whether among its black leaders or white, the degree of fortitude, endurance, and initiative that has been manifested by them for their people's good, that you realize something of the quality of this gift to the African people. If you look back to the sheer heroism of the early days—to Wilson or to Mackay, alone in their equatorial solitude; to the native, whether chief, or teacher, or peasant, who stood by them in the fire of persecution, you are stirred to thanksgiving. If in more recent days, you pause to look into the later product, here in Central Africa, of an ecclesiastical system complete in almost all its parts, administered, in spite of every obstacle, so smoothly and so effectively, not by Europeans only, but by native clergy and teachers no less, it is again to wonder and to thank God.

But, as the present Bishop of Uganda so rightly warns us : " The magnitude of the apparent success must not blind us to its inevitable limitations." " One cannot," says Albert Lloyd, " ignore the dark side of the picture. It is true that in the Uganda Church there is to-day a very dark side which fills all workers out here with serious apprehension."[1] The moral evolution of an African tribe must needs be frightfully difficult. Heredity and environment are both yoked in fierce antagonism to progress. Given even the new and clean atmosphere of a Christian boarding school, the boy and girl find themselves, when the holidays come, and still more when school-days end, back again with the instincts of heredity, fed once more upon the garbage of a vile environment. Young men baptized, and even confirmed, at the age of 18 or 20, find at 30 the pressure of convention overwhelming, and relapse only too easily into polygamy. " The discussion on church discipline which took place in the Synod of 1913 brought the question of national morals prominently to the front. . . . Since that discussion there seems to the casual observer but little improvement in the state of the Church. The two great evils against which there is constant warfare, drunkenness and immorality, are as flagrant as ever; indeed the latter is more open to the world than ever it was. Plurality of wives and concubinage are everywhere, and the whole Church is riddled with this sin, while drunkenness follows in its train."[2] "The wages of sin is

[1] " Dayspring in Uganda," p. 112.   [2] *Ibid.*, p. 112.

death." The outcome of carnal living and thinking is a dying of enthusiasm and will-power. It is a deadening contagion in the sphere of the spirit which saps away the true life of the community. All the members suffer. "*Sebo, tufude* (Sir, we are dead)," was the terse epitome of the situation by a native clergyman, come recently to work in a district of exceptional difficulty. There is something infinitely pathetic in this re-engulfing into the slough of a tribe that has made real efforts to rise out of it. And none feel it more poignantly than do the native Christian leaders themselves. Frequent are their conferences and prayers in the quest of right living. Africa awaits to-day a new kind of leadership from within.

I have tried to sketch in more than one portrait of an African clergyman. I have endeavoured to depict Apolo, prince of missionaries, with his flock gathered in from the shy peoples of the Belgian Congo; Kezekiya among his mountain congregations on Elgon; Sira Dongo and his Acholi people; Fesito with his boys at Mengo Central School. I love to think of others: one, gentle and contemplative, was a frequent companion and correspondent; another, brisk and business-like, an excellent organizer;

a third, reserved but effective—each with a strong sense of responsibility and a real pastoral instinct. I am left full of admiration for many of my black brethren in the ministry. To multiply such native clergy, of true character, must be ever the first care of a living mission. The clergy of Africa vary in character and temperament precisely as do the clergy of England. They are men of like passions with ourselves. They are quickly susceptible to the influences around them. They vary similarly in their capacity or readiness to accept the higher life. And whereas day and night in many parts they are girt about with traditions and customs the most degrading imaginable, it is little wonder that even with their long probation they are not all patterns to their flocks. How to train them, how to protect them, how to keep them in living touch with their divine Head, this is the primary problem.

Mukono is the training college of the Uganda ministry. The position is singularly gracious. Some eighteen miles out of the capital upon the Kampala-Jinja road, it stands upraised upon the slope of a hill, its large central quadrangle falling away from the fine central block of buildings upon the highest side. There are chapel, offices, lecture-room, and library. North and east are the dormitories, each man having his own cubicle. Below, between the college buildings and the road, are the playing fields. Above are the bungalows of the European staff. The college is the Uganda memorial to Bishop Tucker. The dormitories individually commemorate the great names of Mackay, Pilkington, and Walker, and in what manner could the labours of these, who so fearlessly and faithfully planted the Cross, better be perpetuated than in this provision for the rearing of a Christian ministry from among those natives themselves for whom they spent their lives.

Here it is that Canon Daniell exercises his firm yet gentle sway over his three groups of eager students. The juniors are those ready for the certificate of a second-grade catechist—the Bishop's "second letter," as it is called. The middle group are those who are up for their "third letter," which admits them to the highest grade of catechist or teacher. The seniors are those studying for the diaconate. Before each step in this upward course intervenes a period of at least two years of pastoral work. No sinecure this; for before any can return to Mukono for their next course they must be

Future Leadership

approved, upon the merit of such pastoral activity, by their ruridecanal conference, who find the money for their college fees. The training for the " first letter " is undertaken locally in each district.

As an organization this teacher scheme in Uganda is remarkable. Planted upon that apparently innate instinct of the African for teaching, you find to-day at work in Uganda alone some 4500 Christian teachers, one to every 660 people—even counting the outlying districts where teachers are few. Upon this body is raised the teacher scheme, kept quick and effective by the demand for training, which is always far in excess of the possible supply; and centralized again remarkably by the circumstance that from the remotest districts men of widely variant tribes and tongues come recurrently to this one clergy school of the diocese, whether they are to be lifelong catechists or whether ultimately they will attain to the priesthood itself. The long period of training, usually extending to twelve years, offers, moreover, valuable moral securities. In spite of frightful temptation and inducements of the strongest kind, it is a wonderful tribute to this system to admit that with a few distressing exceptions those who attain to the higher grades have proved themselves loyal to the apostolic injunction to be the husband of one wife.

The defects of such a training scheme are evident. It involves a "peasant priesthood." The selection of clergy in the main from the ranks of the *bakopi* (peasants) as distinct from the families of the chiefs tends, whatever their character, to impair their influence. And the long-drawn-out succession of teaching grades means that the priesthood is rather an ultimate reward for long and faithful service than a vocation in itself. It is in consequence all the more notable that Canon Daniell, with the material at his command, should be able to show the results he does. To stay for a day or two at Mukono as his guest is to discover the spirit of the place. The early African morning, that turns every dewy blade of grass to diamonds, and fills the far Kyagwe distance with a soft haze, finds you in the chapel. Noiselessly the building fills and whitens, as the men in their white kanzus take their places in rows barefooted upon the mats. A student reads the lessons. The Principal takes the prayers. Breakfast follows at the bungalow above, and after breakfast come the lectures for the day.

The blackboard must be freely used, the " points " of the lecture written up and dictated. These are men who, whatever their cerebral limitations (and the African brain is still something of a mystery), are eager to learn. They are men, too, who after years of teaching know their Bible. The difficulty there, as at home, is to deduce from the old setting of Scripture the new and living conception of the Kingdom to be built up on earth to-day. They have, moreover, no apparent interest in the history of their continent, nor of its earlier prominence, whether in Carthage or Alexandria or Abyssinia, in the Church's story. Their conception of art and beauty is of the slightest. Still, it is stimulating to the lecturer to meet with their quick response to some of the deepest questions of Christian doctrine, and to realize their familiarity with the scripture narrative.

In two directions the Mukono course calls for fuller sympathy and support. The English language—that in earlier days imported, no doubt, an alien note—should now, for sufficient reasons, be taught to every student at Mukono : first as a *lingua franca*, and then, if one may say so, as a *lingua theologica*. The African undoubtedly needs a tribal speech to preserve his domestic intercourse and to conserve his sentiment for his own people. He needs also to-day a brotherhood speech to affiliate him with the larger world outside. Fifty years ago Swahili might reasonably have been selected, as indeed Alexander Mackay once urged for this purpose. It is not the least startling of the many indications of the march of affairs that English is now at least an equal to Swahili in this respect, and will soon surpass it. If the British doctor can now lecture to his black medical students in English, if the British engineer can speak English to his black mechanics, it is unfortunate that the clergy, who should be the most learned body in the country, are debarred by their linguistic ignorance from similar educational contacts. Learning and piety must ever be the twin requirements for the Christian ministry, not in Europe alone, but universally. The black clergyman should be among the first to open intercourse with the young missionary who has come out to help him. He needs English, moreover, not only on the grounds of learning, but of piety. The devotional works, translated even into Luganda, are inevitably few. If the African ministry is to grow in grace, it must have access to that field of homely piety that is to be found nowhere so richly as in the religious publications that for generations have emerged from England for the help of devout minds.

It is this devotional side of the pastor's office that calls, like his language study, for fuller sympathy and instruction. "Not to win numbers to a Church, but to win them to the Saviour." If Mackay's words are sorely needed for ourselves of the missionary body, they are no less so for our African brethren, on whom is devolving steadily an increasing oversight of the flock of God. According to the latest statistics (1925) there are in the Diocese of Uganda some 165,771 baptized persons. To shepherd them there are but seventy-one clergy. In Teso, to take one separate district, just under 20,000 are either baptized or under instruction for baptism, and there are only four native clergy. There are, besides, in the schools of Teso another 22,000 pupils. The tendency therefore is for the clergy to be so absorbed with the preparation of their classes for baptism and Confirmation, and their numerous duties in the way of preaching, travelling, and organization, that the care of the post-confirmed—the primary concern of a watchful pastor—is neglected ;

and the whole Church suffers in consequence. Native clergy should be trained from their college days to the systematic care of their confirmed members. John Wesley used to declare that to build up the converted one week-day class was a necessity. And it would mean much to the Church in Uganda if the clergy felt it to be an integral part of their duty to hold communicant preparation services, and " Wednesday evening" instruction services, or some such week-day gatherings, as have proved themselves to belong to the best evangelical traditions in England. Good, too, would it be for the devotional life of these native pastors if they could embrace, as a great spiritual provision hallowed by the use of the Church in all ages, the principle of daily morning and evening prayer. The Uganda Prayer Book lays it down that they are to read daily Morning and Evening Prayer and " to cause a drum to be beaten thereunto." On Namirembe the "prayer drum" is duly beaten each evening, but the assembly for prayer has fallen into desuetude. Its restoration, for the whole Church's sake, but especially for the clergy's sake, is much to be wished.

From this vantage-point of our first jubilee we look across the years to that

Future Leadership 247

centenary which, if the Lord tarry, is our next great landmark in the process of time. There is yet much land to be occupied. There is yet much of increase and development and recovery needed. What will those who succeed us have then to record of the little army of African Christians who will have come out, whether as teachers or medical assistants or secretaries or clergy, at the call of their people's need? Will they have to tell on this eastern side of a qualified doctor? Of some schoolmaster or clergyman with a recognized degree, of some outstanding leader raised to the episcopate? One thing is certain. By reason of his dependent nature the African will still need the spiritual arm of his white brother in the Church's ministry. And by all the law of brotherhood it will still be the duty of the white brother to offer it to him to the utmost of his power. Already in the highly civilized Church of Japan, wherein two Japanese bishops have been consecrated, the question has arisen. Do they desire, or do they not, the further assistance of the British clergy? Formally, through an episcopal emissary, the question was asked of them by the head of the Anglican Church. Without equivocation the answer has been sent : " Yes, we need them, if not for administration, most certainly for devotional support." Such will still be the need of Uganda—" not to win numbers to a Church, but to win men to the Saviour." Mackay's appeal will ring out still. So far as ever the eye can pierce the future, clergy will be needed, teachers will be needed, doctors will be needed, nurses will be needed, to instruct, to advise, to superintend, above all to inspire the growing native Church.

Conditions of missionary service will change. The rapid growth of communications, the pressure of imperial opportunities, the desirability of closer international relationships must steadily bring about new conceptions in the Church itself. The deep gulf between the home Church and the Church overseas, if not done away, will be adequately spanned. The " world oneness," so widely preached, will awaken some answering " Church oneness." It will cease to be an eccentric thing, it will become a natural thing for a clergyman to spend some part at least of his ministry among Asiatic or African peoples. That inter-racial *bonhomie* which the world so sorely needs will find the clergy of a universal Church to be its most practical exponents.

Future Leadership

The woman's movement, still in its infancy, still marred in certain directions by over-exuberance, still cramped in others by an unnecessary suspicion, will discipline itself, so it would seem, during the next fifty years into a mighty, world-redeeming force. In this loud " World Call " the voices of the women, even of the backward races, are insistent. These mothers of the Africa that is to be are at last making their wants known, and with the coming of a more generous trust in the goodness and capacity of our women workers will come the needed response. This is no jubilee of English women's work in Central Africa. It is but its coming of age. Yet already tribe after tribe has felt through the school or dispensary, or the tour of itineration, the touch of a white woman's hand, and often the warmth and strength of her friendship. If these twenty-one years have produced so much, what will the next fifty have in store ?

What will not change will be that essential something in the African that continually cries out for stability and for peace. To those of us who have lived with him in his own land there are certain of his characteristics that yield memories of the happiest kind. We have travelled with him, we have worked with him, we have played with him, we have served on committees with him, we have prayed with him. We have enjoyed his unstinted hospitality, his shrewdness, his abundant humour, his deep capacity for spiritual things. We have appreciated his standard of cleanliness, his love of order. As a servant he has been one of our best friends. To know him is to grow fond of him. It is also to know more and more poignantly the pathos of his inheritance and the frequent pathos of his environment, the sorrow of his passions and of his sins. It is to know his baffling agony in the gulf that so often lies between his desires and his attainments. " Lord, Thou knowest that we have all fallen back : there is none that is living according to Thy commands "— I do not forget that teacher's prayer of penitence on Mount Elgon. These people cry aloud for that pardon which is only adequate because divine. " Do you ever use the word ' propitiation ' ? " I asked once of one of them. The word in Luganda is *mutango*. " Yes," he said ; " every Monday in the *baraza*." And he explained. The *baraza* is the court, and Monday is court day, and the *mutango* is the penalty

Future Leadership

awarded. " Have you ever," I asked, " been taught that in all reverence we may use that word of our Redeemer ? " " Yes, that is what we have been taught." " And do you believe it ? " " We do." The great gospel of the Atonement—still to the intellectual, foolishness, and to the prejudiced, a stumbling block—is to the African life. With all his limitations, this gospel of pardon and of power, this hope of liberation and of moral strength, is something that this backward man can grasp. There will be no change in his need of divine grace. And there will be no change in the Will of God that he should receive it. It is when we see, as some of us have seen it, this onward march of the Church of Christ among peoples the most unlikely and into regions the most remote; into the pygmy forest it may be on the one frontier or among the mountain tribes of Elgon on the other, among the shy Acholi to the north or the people of Ruanda far away to the south—it is then we know of a surety that this thing is of God.

Fifty years ago a solitary Englishman stood alone at Mengo as His witness. To-day, radiating from that same centre, hundreds of thousands of simple Africans claim to be adherents of His Church. North and south, east and west, beyond the advances of any white evangelist, African has enlisted African in the great fellowship of Christ. Crude and imperfect no doubt has been the presentation of the gospel message, frail and variable its acceptance. Make, however, what deductions you will, this shining out of the light of Christianity at the heart of the dark continent constitutes one of the crowning wonders of our generation. No human explanation will meet the whole case. We are lifted up to see something that has exceeded man's highest expectation. Here once again is an epiphany that postulates, not questioning, but worship. One attitude only suffices. *Non nobis Domine.* Not unto us, O Lord, but unto Thy Name give the praise. To Him that is able to do exceeding abundantly above all that we asked or thought, to Him be the glory.

And if this be so, one thing further follows: As we look out upon the means used to secure this great achievement—upon the endurance, the wisdom, the zeal, but most of all the endurance, by which it has been reached—we are compelled to pay some tribute of an exceptional kind to the long array of men and women who down these fifty years have accomplished it. Such an ascription would be very far from their desires. Rather would they with one voice declare that all that they have given only adds to the measure of their joy in such service. If this onward march of the Church be of God, if this ever-increasing stream be part of His purpose of love in the redemption of the world, then for them it follows, and for all that hidden host of intercessors and fellow-labourers who from afar have sustained them, that it must be the supreme honour of their lives to have had some share in so glorious an expansion.

APPENDIX I

SOME NOTABLE DATES IN THE HISTORY OF UGANDA

1505 Portuguese East African Empire began.
1698 Arabs expel Portuguese from East Africa.
1848 Kenya and Kilima-njaro discovered by Krapf and Rebmann.
1860 Speke and Grant establish Lake Victoria as the main source of the Nile, visit Uganda, and follow the Nile down to Cairo.
1864 Samuel Baker discovers Lake Albert.
1873 Death of Livingstone.
1875 H. M. Stanley visits Uganda.
  Stanley's challenge and C.M.S. response.
1877 First two missionaries reach Uganda.
1878 Mackay arrives in Uganda.
1879 First R.C. missionaries reach Uganda.
  Uganda sends envoys to England.
1882 First baptisms in Uganda.
  Hannington sails for Uganda.
1884 Beginning of the scramble for Africa.
  Consecration of Bishop Hannington.
  Death of King Mtesa: accession of Mwanga.
1885 Persecution begins in Uganda.
  Murder of Bishop Hannington.
1886 Consecration of Bishop Parker.
1888 British East Africa Company incorporated.
  Death of Bishop Parker.
  Civil War in Uganda; Mwanga dethroned.
1889 Mwanga restored.
1890 Death of Mackay.
  Consecration of Bishop Tucker.
  Passing of Brussels Act.
1891 B.E.A. Company decide to give up Uganda.
  Bishop Tucker's appeal and C.M.S. response.
1893 British Protectorate proclaimed at Mengo.
  Agreement among Baganda chiefs to abolish slavery.

	First Baganda clergy ordained.
	Beginnings of missionary work outside Buganda.
1895	First women missionaries reach Uganda.
1897	Civil War in Uganda.
	Death of Pilkington.
	Diocése of Uganda formed.
1899	Mwanga deported : accession of King Daudi.
1900	Uganda Settlement concluded between Sir H. Johnston and kingdom of Buganda.
1901	Uganda Railway reaches Lake Victoria.
	Work begun in Ankole.
1904	First brick Cathedral consecrated.
1908	Work begun in Teso.
1911	Retirement of Bishop Tucker.
1912	Consecration of Bishop Willis.
1913	First Synod of the Church.
1919	Present Cathedral consecrated.
1926	Creation of the Diocese of Upper Nile.

APPENDIX II
BISHOPS AND ADMINISTRATORS, UGANDA

BISHOPS OF EASTERN EQUATORIAL AFRICA
(Including Uganda)

Hannington, James	1884–5
Parker, Henry Perrott	1886–8
Tucker, Alfred Robert	1890–7

BISHOPS OF UGANDA

Tucker, Alfred Robert	1897–1911
Willis, John Jamieson	1912

BISHOP OF THE UPPER NILE

Kitching, Arthur Leonard	1926

ADMINISTRATORS

COMMISSIONERS

Col. Colville	1893
E. J. L. Berkeley, Esq.	1895
Sir H. H. Johnston	1899
Lt.-Col. Sir J. Hayes Sadler	1901

GOVERNORS

Sir H. H. Bell	1905
Major H. E. S. Cordeaux (never assumed office)	1909
Sir F. J. Jackson	1911
Sir R. T. Coryndon	1918
Sir Geoffrey Archer	1923
Sir W. F. Gowers	1925

APPENDIX III
ROLL OF THOSE WHO HAVE SERVED IN THE UGANDA MISSION

*Denotes those who have served as laymen. †Denotes doctors.

1876
*Mackay, A. M.
*O'Neill, T.
*Robertson, W. M.
*Robertson, J.
*Smith, Lieut. G. Shergold (R.N.)
†*Smith, J.
Wilson, C. T.

1877
†*Baxter, E. J.
*Copplestone, A. J.
*Sneath, G. E.
*Tytherleigh, W. C.

1878
*Felkin, R. W.
*Hall, J. W.
Litchfield, G.
*Pearson, C. W.
*Stokes, C.

1880
*Biddlecombe, A. J.
O'Flaherty, P.

1882
Ashe, R. P.
Blackburn, J.
Edmonds, W. J.
Gordon, E. C.
Hannington, J. (Consecrated Bishop in Equatorial Africa, 1884).
*Wise, C.

1884
*Jeanes, H. W.
Roscoe, J.

1885
*Hooper, D. A. L.

1886
Parker, H. P. (Bishop in Equatorial Africa).

1887
*Deekes, D.
Walker, R. H. (Archdeacon of Uganda, 1892).

1890
Baskerville, G. K. (Archdeacon of Uganda, 1912).
*Cotter, J. D.
Dermott, J. V.
Dunn, J. W.
Hill, J. W. H.
*Hunt, H. J.
*Pilkington, G. L.
*Smith, F. C.
Tucker, A. R. (Bishop of Equatorial Africa, 1890; Bishop of Uganda, 1897).

1891
*Collins, W.
Crabtree, W. A.
Greaves, G. H. V.
*Gunther, C. A.
Hubbard, E. H.
†*Wright, Gaskoin R. M.

1892
Fisher, A. B.
Leakey, R. H.
Millar, E.
*Nickisson, J. P.

1893
*Fletcher, T. B.
Rowling, F.
Sugden, H. R.

1894
Blackledge, G. R. (Archdeacon of Uganda, 1926).
Lewin, H. B.
Lloyd, A. B. (Archdeacon of Western Uganda, 1921).
Pike, A. J.

1895
Browne, Miss E. E. (Mrs. Rowling).
Buckley, T. R. (Archdeacon of Busoga, 1908, and of Kavirondo, 1912).
Chadwick, Miss J. E.

Furley, Miss E. M.
Hall, M. J.
Pilgrim, Miss E. L.
Purvis, J. B.
Thomsett, Miss M. S.
Wilson, A.
Wright, F. H.

1896
Bird, Miss G. E.
Callis, J. S.
Clayton, H.
†*Cook, A. R.
Taylor, Miss B. (Mrs. H. E. Maddox).
Tegart, H. W.
Timpson, Miss K. (Mrs. A. R. Cook).
Weatherhead, H. W.
*Whitehouse, A.
Wigram, B. E.

1897
*Borup, K. E.
Ecob, C. H. T.
*Force-Jones, R.
*Hattersley, C. W.
Maddox, H. E.

1898
Crabtree, Mrs. W. A.
Gordon, Mrs. E. C.
Skeens, S. R.

1899
Casson, G. H.
†*Cook, J. H., and Mrs.
*Farthing, H. H.
*Innes, W. G. S., and Mrs.
Leakey, Mrs. R. H.
Lloyd, Mrs. A. B.
Pike, Miss E. C.
Purser, J. W.
Scott, Miss H. D. I. (Mrs. G. R. Blackledge).
Tanner, Miss S. R. (Mrs. S. R. Skeens).

1900
Allen, Miss A. E.
*Davies, E. C.
*Fraser, A. G.

Glass, Miss A. B. (Mrs. A. G. Fraser).
Hurditch, Miss R. (Mrs. A. B. Fisher).
*Kemp, A. W.
*Phillips, C. J.
Robinson, Miss A. H.
*Savile, H. O.
Weatherhead, H. T. C.
Willis, J. J. (Consecrated Bishop of Uganda, 1912).

1901
Allen, Miss A. L.
†*Bond, Ashton, and Mrs.
Brewer, Miss E. M.
Chadwick, W. (Archdeacon of Kavirondo, 1915).
Dallison, Miss B. E. (Mrs. H. G. Dillistone).
Dillistone, H. G.
Dyke, Miss T. L.
Johnson, T. B.
Kitching, A. L. (Consecrated Bishop of the Upper Nile, 1926).
O'Connor, D. A.
Thomas, Miss H. M. (Mrs. A. Bond).
Turnbull, Miss H. M. (Mrs. H. Clayton).
Weatherhead, Mrs. H. W.
Wright, Mrs. F. H.

1902
Baker, Miss M. T.
Barton, Miss K. E. (Mrs. H. O. Savile).
Baskerville, Mrs. G. K.
Daniell, E. S.
Owrid, T.

1903
Attlee, Miss A. K.
Ecob, Mrs. C. H. T.
Hannington, J. E. M.
Hattersley, Mrs. C. W.
Jacob, Miss A. A. (Mrs. J. Britton).
Ladbury, H. B., and Mrs.
Mathers, H. (Archdeacon of Eastern Province, 1923).

Appendix

Ostler, Miss M.
Purvis, Mrs. J. B.
Walton, Miss L. O. (Mrs. W. E. Owen).

1904
Gill, W. B.
Hattersley, Miss E.
Herbert, J. S.
Hill, Miss E. T.
Holdgate, Miss H. F.
Owen, W. E. (Archdeacon of Kavirondo, 1904, Mombasa Diocese, 1921).
Piffin, Miss E. M.
Pleydell, A. E.
Reed, Miss F. K.
Taylor, Miss M. A.

1905
Brewer, H. A.
Casson, Mrs. G. H.
*Gerber, M.
*Holden, W.
Wright, H. T.

1906
Barry, Miss M. L. R. (Mrs. H. A. Brewer).
Brown, Miss M.
Burden, C. J. A.
Coombs, Miss W. L. (Mrs. H. Mathers).
Hannington, Mrs. J. E. M.
Leech, A. J.
McNamara, Miss I. S. (Mrs. A. J. Leech).
Morris, Miss A. M. (Mrs. H. K. Banks).
Welsh, Miss A. J.
Wilson, Mrs. A.

1907
Bowers, H., and Mrs.
Britton, J.
Flint, Miss G. M. (Mrs. T. R. Buckley).
Kitching, Mrs. A. L.
Moore, Miss L. H. (Mrs. W. B. Gill).
Owen, Mrs. W. E.
Tegart, Mrs. H. W.

1908
Banks, H. K.
Bingham, Miss L. M.
Fergusson, Miss I. (Mrs. H. B. Lewin).
Herbert, Mrs. J. S.
Mathew, Miss A. M.

1909
Burden, Mrs. C. J. A.
Gordon, Miss R. F.
Owrid, Mrs. T.
Smyth, Miss C. J.
Syson, W. S., and Mrs.
Weatherhead, Mrs. H. T. C.

1910
†*Cook, E. N.
Holden, Mrs. W.
Phillips, Mrs. C. J.
Russell, W. S. R.
Walker, Mrs. R. H.
Watney, Miss C.
*White, F. H.
Wright, Miss H. F.

1911
Brown, Miss A. M.
Pleydell, Mrs. A. E.
Skelton, Miss E. M.

1912
Daniell, Mrs. E. S.
Godfrey, Miss M. I.

1913
Garrett, G. G., and Mrs.
Harvey, Miss A. Y. (Mrs. J. Britton).
*Hunt, J. S., and Mrs.
Lees, P. H.
McMinn, Miss S.

1914
Davies, Miss B. M. (Mrs. W. B. Lea-Wilson).
Downer, Miss E. B.
Gem, Miss C. E. C. H.
Grace, H. M.
Lang, Miss R. van H.
Patmore, Miss A. E.
Rogers, F. S.
†*Sharp, L. E. S.
Wilson, Mrs. A.

Appendix

1915
Brittain, Miss E. R.
Cook, Mrs. E. N.
Couch, Miss D. E. (Mrs. P. H. Lees).
Ensor, Miss M.
Latham, S. B.
Lawrence, T. L.
Russell, Mrs. W. S. R.
White, Mrs. F. H.

1916
Cook, Miss E. M. (Mrs. J. H. Robinson).
Hamlyn, Miss K. I.
Hornby, Miss C.
Kitching, Mrs. A. L.
Miller, Miss M. M. (Mrs. H. T. Wright).
Pitt Pitts, W. A.

1917
*Hoyle, W. E., and Mrs.
†*Smith, A. C. Stanley

1918
Clarke, A. E.
Leakey, Miss I. M. B.

1919
Budd, Miss M. S.
Foster Smith, Miss D. M.
Smith, Mrs. A. C. S.

1920
Ainley, Miss N. E.
Allshorn, Miss F.
Cave, Miss J.
Gooseman, Miss G.
Grace, Mrs. H. M.
Hirst, J. C., and Mrs.
Jones, H. Gresford (Bishop of Kampala), and Mrs.
Marshall, Miss E.
Muller, Miss K.
Reeves, Miss D. B.
Rogers, Mrs. F. S.
Sharp, Mrs. L. E. S.

1921
Biggs, Miss F. A.
Garrard, Miss E. R. J.
Gibbings, Miss C. M.
†*Hunter, E. V., and Mrs.
†*Macdonald, A. H., and Mrs.
*Robinson, J. F.

1922
Pitt Pitts, Mrs. W. A.

1923
Ainley, Miss E. H.
*Callwell, Commander E. W. E. (R.N.).
Camplin, Miss R.
Martin, Miss B. S.
Mitton, F., and Mrs.
†*Schofield, A. T.
White, Miss L. S.

1924
Guyler, Miss H. M.
*Holmes, G.
Lawrence, Mrs. T. L.
Lyon, Miss S.
Rowe, Miss E. F.
Warren, J. E. L.
Willis, Mrs. J. J.

1925
†Ardell, Miss K.
Armitage, Miss G. E. (Mrs. A. T. Schofield).
Banks, Miss N. E.
Cafe, Miss E. L.
Cochrane, Miss H. M.
Davies, H. F.
Robinson, Miss R. E.
†*Stones, R. Y., and Mrs.
Vincent, T. C. L.
Wheeler, A. W.

1926
Allan, Miss D. I.
†*Church, J. E.
Drakeley, Miss C. M.
Ibbotson, Miss D. E.
Jackson, H. S.
Linton, Miss P.
Sadler, Miss M.
Salisbury, Miss M. L.
Skipper, Miss T. M.
Wild, Miss M. A.

APPENDIX IV

RECENT BOOKS ON UGANDA

Handbook of the Uganda Protectorate.
 Admiralty. H.M. Stationery Office. 1921

Twenty-Five Years in Central Africa.
 J. Roscoe. Cambridge University Press. 1921

Dayspring in Uganda. A. B. Lloyd. C.M.S. 1921

The King of the Snakes.
 Folk-lore Stories from Uganda. Rosetta Baskerville. C.M.S. 1922

The Soul of Central Africa.
 A general Report of the Mackie Ethnological Expedition to Central Africa. J. Roscoe. Cassell and Co. 1922

The Bakitara of Banyoro.
 The first part of the Report of the Mackie Ethnological Expedition to Central Africa. J. Roscoe. Cambridge University Press. 1923

The Banyankole.
 The second part of the Report of the Mackie Ethnological Expedition to Central Africa. J. Roscoe. Cambridge University Press. 1923

The Partition and Colonization of Africa.
 Sir Charles Lucas. Clarendon Press, Oxford. 1923

The Dual Mandate in British Tropical Africa.
 Sir F. D. Lugard. Blackwood. 1923

The Lango : A Nilotic Tribe of Uganda.
J. H. Driberg. 1923

Apolo of the Pygmy Forest.
A. B. Lloyd. C.M.S. 1924

The Bagesu and Other Tribes of the Uganda Protectorate.
The third part of the Report of the Mackie Ethnological Expedition to Central Africa. J. Roscoe. Cambridge University Press. 1924

Education in East Africa.
The Report of the Phelps Stokes Commission. Edinburgh House Press. 1925

An African Church in Building.
The Bishop of Uganda. C.M.S. 1925

The Flame Tree.
More Folk-lore Stories from Uganda. Rosetta Baskerville. C.M.S. 1925

Tales of Uganda. Various writers. C.M.S. 1926

Related Titles from Westphalia Press

The Limits of Moderation: Jimmy Carter and the Ironies of American Liberalism

The Limits of Moderation: Jimmy Carter and the Ironies of American Liberalism is not a finished product. And yet, even in this unfinished stage, this book is a close and careful history of a short yet transformative period in American political history, when big changes were afoot.

The Zelensky Method
by Grant Farred

Locating Russian's war within a global context, The Zelensky Method is unsparing in its critique of those nations, who have refused to condemn Russia's invasion and are doing everything they can to prevent economic sanctions from being imposed on the Kremlin.

Sinking into the Honey Trap: The Case of the Israeli-Palestinian Conflict
by Daniel Bar-Tal, Barbara Doron, Translator

Sinking into the Honey Trap by Daniel Bar-Tal discusses how politics led Israel to advancing the occupation, and of the deterioration of democracy and morality that accelerates the growth of an authoritarian regime with nationalism and religiosity.

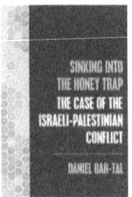

Essay on The Mysteries and the True Object of The Brotherhood of Freemasons
by Jason Williams

The third edition of Essai sur les mystères discusses Freemasonry's role as a society of symbolic philosophers who cultivate their minds, practice virtues, and engage in charity, and underscores the importance of brotherhood, morality, and goodwill.

Bunker Diplomacy: An Arab-American in the U.S. Foreign Service
by Nabeel Khoury

After twenty-five years in the Foreign Service, Dr. Nabeel A. Khoury retired from the U.S. Department of State in 2013 with the rank of Minister Counselor. In his last overseas posting, Khoury served as deputy chief of mission at the U.S. embassy in Yemen (2004-2007).

Managing Challenges for the Flint Water Crisis
Edited by Toyna E. Thornton, Andrew D. Williams, Katherine M. Simon, Jennifer F. Sklarew

This edited volume examines several public management and intergovernmental failures, with particular attention on social, political, and financial impacts. Understanding disaster meaning, even causality, is essential to the problem-solving process.

User-Centric Design
by Dr. Diane Stottlemyer

User-centric strategy can improve by using tools to manage performance using specific techniques. User-centric design is based on and centered around the users. They are an essential part of the design process and should have a say in what they want and need from the application based on behavior and performance.

Masonic Myths and Legends
by Pierre Mollier

Freemasonry is one of the few organizations whose teaching method is still based on symbols. It presents these symbols by inserting them into legends that are told to its members in initiation ceremonies. But its history itself has also given rise to a whole mythology.

Abortion and Informed Common Sense
by Max J. Skidmore

The controversy over a woman's "right to choose," as opposed to the numerous "rights" that abortion opponents decide should be assumed to exist for "unborn children," has always struck me as incomplete. Two missing elements of the argument seems obvious, yet they remain almost completely overlooked.

The Athenian Year Primer: Attic Time-Reckoning and the Julian Calendar
by Christopher Planeaux

The ability to translate ancient Athenian calendar references into precise Julian-Gregorian dates will not only assist Ancient Historians and Classicists to date numerous historical events with much greater accuracy but also aid epigraphists in the restorations of numerous Attic inscriptions.

Siddhartha: Life of the Buddha
by David L. Phillips,
contributions by Venerable Sitagu Sayadaw

Siddhartha: Life of the Buddha is an illustrated story for adults and children about the Buddha's birth, enlightenment and work for social justice. It includes illustrations from Pagan, Burma which are provided by Rev. Sitagu Sayadaw.

Growing Inequality: Bridging Complex Systems, Population Health, and Health Disparities
Editors: George A. Kaplan, Ana V. Diez Roux, Carl P. Simon, and Sandro Galea

Why is America's health is poorer than the health of other wealthy countries and why health inequities persist despite our efforts? In this book, researchers report on groundbreaking insights to simulate how these determinants come together to produce levels of population health and disparities and test new solutions.

Issues in Maritime Cyber Security
Edited by Dr. Joe DiRenzo III, Dr. Nicole K. Drumhiller, and Dr. Fred S. Roberts

The complexity of making MTS safe from cyber attack is daunting and the need for all stakeholders in both government (at all levels) and private industry to be involved in cyber security is more significant than ever as the use of the MTS continues to grow.

Female Emancipation and Masonic Membership: An Essential Collection
By Guillermo De Los Reyes Heredia

Female Emancipation and Masonic Membership: An Essential Combination is a collection of essays on Freemasonry and gender that promotes a transatlantic discussion of the study of the history of women and Freemasonry and their contribution in different countries.

Anti-Poverty Measures in America: Scientism and Other Obstacles
Editors, Max J. Skidmore and Biko Koenig

Anti-Poverty Measures in America brings together a remarkable collection of essays dealing with the inhibiting effects of scientism, an over-dependence on scientific methodology that is prevalent in the social sciences, and other obstacles to anti-poverty legislation.

Geopolitics of Outer Space: Global Security and Development
by Ilayda Aydin

A desire for increased security and rapid development is driving nation-states to engage in an intensifying competition for the unique assets of space. This book analyses the Chinese-American space discourse from the lenses of international relations theory, history and political psychology to explore these questions.

Contests of Initiative: Countering China's Gray Zone Strategy in the East and South China Seas
by Dr. Raymond Kuo

China is engaged in a widespread assertion of sovereignty in the South and East China Seas. It employs a "gray zone" strategy: using coercive but sub-conventional military power to drive off challengers and prevent escalation, while simultaneously seizing territory and asserting maritime control.

Discourse of the Inquisitive
Editors: Jaclyn Maria Fowler and Bjorn Mercer

Good communication skills are necessary for articulating learning, especially in online classrooms. It is often through writing that learners demonstrate their ability to analyze and synthesize the new concepts presented in the classroom.

westphaliapress.org

Policy Studies Organization

The Policy Studies Organization (PSO) is a publisher of academic journals and book series, sponsor of conferences, and producer of programs.

Policy Studies Organization publishes dozens of journals on a range of topics, such as European Policy Analysis, Journal of Elder Studies, Indian Politics & Polity, Journal of Critical Infrastructure Policy, and Popular Culture Review.

Additionally, Policy Studies Organization hosts numerous conferences. These conferences include the Middle East Dialogue, Space Education and Strategic Applications Conference, International Criminology Conference, Dupont Summit on Science, Technology and Environmental Policy, World Conference on Fraternalism, Freemasonry and History, and the Internet Policy & Politics Conference.

For more information on these projects, access videos of past events, and upcoming events, please visit us at:

www.ipsonet.org

www.ingramcontent.com/pod-product-compliance
Lightning Source LLC
Chambersburg PA
CBHW052134070526
44585CB00017B/1814